NATIONAL PARK MYSTERIES & DISAPPEARANCES VOLUME 2

CALIFORNIA (YOSEMITE, JOSHUA TREE, MOUNT SHASTA)

STEVE STOCKTON

BILL MELDER

Copyright © 2021 Steve Stockton, Bill Melder
Published by: Beyond The Fray Publishing

This book or any portion thereof may not be reproduced or used in any manner whatsoever without the express written permission of the publisher except for the use of brief quotations in a book review. All rights reserved.

ISBN 13: 978-1-954528-13-0

Cover design: Disgruntled Dystopian Publications

Beyond The Fray Publishing, a division of Beyond The Fray, LLC, San Diego, CA
www.beyondthefraypublishing.com

BEYOND THE FRAY
Publishing

INTRODUCTION

California. The very name elicits the stuff legends and dreams are made of. Whether the pristine beach at Malibu, Hollywood—seat of the entertainment industry and land of movie stars (as well as broken dreams and destroyed lives)—to the desert to the mountains, and everything in between, California has it all. Even those who have never had the pleasure of visiting the Golden State know of it and have preconceived notions brought about by the many portrayals in film and on television.

California, one of the United States' most western states, winds and stretches along the Pacific coast from the border with Mexico to the south, to the border of Oregon to the north. In addition to the entertainment industry in Southern California, you have the Central Valley full of its farmlands, and the Mojave Desert.

Continuing north, more cliff-lined beaches, redwood forests, the hills of San Francisco (with the Golden Gate Bridge, cable cars, and Alcatraz Island) and the Sierra Nevada mountain range.

Yes, California truly does have something for everyone.

But California also has a darker side. Especially in some of its myriad national parks, forests, and wildlife, wilderness, and recreational areas. Strange disappearances where the missing person is not only never found, but nor are any clues. Bizarre stories of cults, sacrifices, and other manner of things happening on public lands. Tales of UFOs, Bigfoot, and haunted places. Still get the same mental imagery when you think of the word "California"?

We're not saying that you shouldn't visit these areas... In fact, for the truly adventurous, these mysterious goings-on are even more incentive to head west to California.

But please use caution. Go prepared or stay home. I don't want to write about you in future updates to this series.

In this volume, we'll be taking an intimate look at three of my favorite (and arguably, strangest) national parks in California: Yosemite, Joshua Tree and Mount Shasta (technically not a national park, but Mount

Shasta is located within the Shasta-Trinity National Forest, which is close enough for our concerns. Mount Shasta is way too weird to be excluded by a park-or-forest designation).

So, buckle up, and join me through a wild ride across the strange, rugged landscape of California. Let us find beautiful monsters there, shall we?

PART 1
YOSEMITE

Yosemite National Park is located in California and nestled snugly in the heart of the Sierra Nevada Mountains. The park was established under federal protection in 1864 and became part of the United States National Park Service on October 1, 1890. Today the park spans more than 740K acres of land and is most well-known for its majestic waterfalls, striking sunsets, and diverse outdoor pursuits that altogether draw more than four million visitors annually. That's a huge park—biggest in California—and a lot of people—it's California's most visited national park.

Yosemite's natural ecosystem supports more than four hundred species of wildlife, including black bear, coyote, and the elusive mountain lion, and its forests are populated by some of the oldest and largest species of trees. The ancient, giant sequoias are the most recognizable big trees of Yosemite, but we can't overlook the sugar pine, especially when it casually drops twenty-four-inch (sixty-one-centimeter) pinecones to the forest floor from heights of over two hundred feet (sixty-one meters). The huge pinecones, dense vegetation, imposing granite mountains, and cascading waterfalls make for a truly remarkable wonderland of natural beauty.

Along with the beautiful surroundings and fun outdoor adventures, Yosemite is burdened with an unfortunate dark side: Mysterious, inexplicable things happen here, and there are a disturbing number of unsolved disappearances from the area, some of which have gone unsolved for decades. Could there be some truth to Yosemite's legends and lore? With so many annual visitors (Yosemite is California's most visited national park, seeing in excess of five million guests per year, it is second only to the Great Smoky Mountains National Park in terms of visitors) and its harsh terrain, a few missing people wouldn't seem uncommon, but the number of disappearances at Yosemite, and within the national park system overall, is beyond unsettling.

In this chapter, we will cover strange events, local

legends, and several very unsettling and unsolved missing persons mysteries from Yosemite National Park, plus a whole lot more. The following events, legends, and disappearances can be frightening, so reader discretion is strongly advised.

CHAPTER ONE

STRANGE EVENTS AT YOSEMITE

Deadly Lightning

Former Yosemite Park ranger John W. Bingaman wrote about several strange events he recalls happening at the park in his 1961 publication titled *Guardians of the Yosemite.*

He begins by saying, "The ranger files of strange accidents through the years reads like a storybook fiction."

The first strange event he covered was about a freak lightning storm that sprang forth unexpectedly. He wrote:

> "... one day a severe lightning storm came up suddenly over Glacier Point when thirty horseback riders were on their way up to the Point. Lightning struck near the

party, and a bolt of fire ran down the trail killing nine saddle horses. The riders fortunately were not injured, only shocked by the charge of lightning so close to them and having their horses killed. No one in the party will ever forget that experience."

It's worth noting that the chance of lightning striking so many living beings at once is exceptionally rare, yet this isn't the only time a "freak" lightning storm has showed up at Yosemite and turned out deadly. Consider these:

In 1985, around 6:30 p.m., five climbers had made their way up to Half Dome overlooking Yosemite Valley and were sitting on top of a cavern. Then, lightning struck the group, killing two of them and injuring the other three (two of them critically). The lightning bolt sent one of the climbers tumbling down four thousand feet.

Sixteen-year-old Brian Gordon was one of the two who passed from fatal injuries, though the identity of the second person who died was withheld until relatives were notified of the incident.

Twenty-eight-year-old Tom Rice and twenty-four-year-old Bruce Weiner were hospitalized at UC Davis Medical Center and were in critical condition from the lightning storm.

Twenty-four-year-old Adrian J. Esteban was treated at the medical center and released the same day.

This event led the National Park Service to issue safety guidelines on how to identify and avoid lightning and thunderstorms at Yosemite. Of course, as these were considered "freak occurrences," all the recognition and avoidance training probably won't be of much benefit. It's a good effort though by the National Park Service, I suppose.

Strange Animal Encounters

Another set of strange events recounted in *Guardians of the Yosemite* by John are a couple of reports of odd coyote behavior.

"Here is another unusual happening," he wrote, "Jeffery Stanton of Walnut Creek, California was camping in the Wawona Camp Ground. Some time during the early morning hours a coyote bit him on the head while he was asleep. He awakened in time to see the coyote trot away into the bushes. First Aid was given and the necessary treatment at the Lewis Memorial hospital for rabies. An extensive hunt by the rangers was made for a week but the coyote was never located and fortunately Mr. Stanton suffered no ill effect from the experience.

"A similar case happened a month later when Karl M. Munson of Yosemite was camping in the Wawona Camp Ground. A coyote or wild dog—or something—scratched him on the head while he was sleeping on the ground. Here again no bad reactions occurred from the experience. But again the rangers hunted for days with no results. It was assumed that the animal was hunting for its food and passed by Karl when he turned or moved in his sleeping bag. The animal may have thought it was something to pounce on as they often do when searching for small game or birds."

John ended the section on strange events he recalled by saying, "These specific accidents are just a few of the many that are reported and treated by rangers as part of a full day's work."

UFO Sighting

On September 19, 2002, during evening hours and just after the sun had set, the visitors of Yosemite were treated to an unexpected visitor—a bright, ball-shaped light in the sky. Also classified as a UFO. The UFO was surrounded by a halo of light much larger than itself, and was trailed by seemingly miles of zigzagging smoke. The ball of light made its way across the sky slowly, and a visitor was able to capture the event on camera before the disk ultimately disappeared into the night.

About thirty minutes after the flying disk went away, the witness writes that air force jets arrived and circled the area multiple times. Nothing unusual was reported. Numerous other incidents like this have happened at Yosemite, and to this day, we don't know for sure what these disks are.

The UFO footage captured that evening in 2002 was regarded as some of the best available for that time. Considering that lightweight camcorders weren't really around and popular until the 1990s, and phone camera recording wasn't around in the US until the early 2000s, it's no surprise.

Yet it seems as though little to no real investigation is being done, or perhaps there's no investigation being publicized, to solve these UFO sightings by identifying what they are, where they originate, and why they appear in the skies.

CHAPTER TWO

YOSEMITE LEGENDS

One might wonder just how are centuries-old tales and legends still around in today's time? It's tempting to think humans should have grown beyond the fear of things that go bump in the night. But despite our current scientific knowledge and advanced technology, some of the most unsettling mysteries we face still go unsolved. Perhaps there's more to those tales of old than meets the eye... Here are just a few of the many legends originating from the Yosemite area.

THE FISH-WOMEN: a Miwok folktale

It is said that thousands of years ago, when the Ah-wah-nee-chees were still a young nation, the Merced

River was the home of the fish-women, or mermaids. These mermaids were beautiful creatures, having the tails of fish, complete with scales and fins, and the upper bodies of gorgeous women. They were unable to leave the water, but would often sit upon the rocks in the shallows, watching, combing their long black hair with loving hands, singing their most alluring of songs to the warriors of Ah-wah-nee. Charming as the mermaids were, the warriors were not easily fooled, and they knew the mermaids were not only very beautiful but very sinister.

One day, there were two braves out fishing in the deep river pools, using a net fashioned with milkweed thread. The net became entangled in the rocks at the bottom of the river. One of the braves dove down to free the netting. This turned out to be an opportunity the fish-women couldn't resist. Once the brave was under the water's surface, the fish-women darted out from under the rocks. They tied the threads of the net to his toes and held him underwater until he drowned. Then, they untied the brave and carried him away to their hidden land beneath the river, and neither the brave nor the mermaids were ever seen again.

THE PO-HO-NO LEGEND

The Miwok Po-ho-no legend holds that Yosemite's Bridalveil Fall is haunted by an ancient, evil spirit that manifests in the form of an alluring and captivating wind.

The story is told of an older woman and a maiden of Ah-wah-nee who were picking berries along the stream above Bridalveil Fall, when something evil happened. As the two were thumbing for the ripest berries, the maiden looked away from her work, down the stream and out toward the brink of the waterfall, where she saw a multicolored mist swirling high into the air.

The maiden was charmed by the beauty of the colors and enchanted by the presence of the mist and the energy it carried. She became further hypnotized until she finally abandoned her hunt for berries altogether and moved down the stream, closer to the swirling colors, and closer to the edge of the falls... Nothing could turn her attention away from the mist—not the older woman calling to her in the background, not even her own self-preservation as she was lured closer to the drop-off. She was focused only on the intoxicating, colorful cloud of mist and wind.

As the maiden took her last few steps toward the brink of the falls, the whirling winds let out a shriek of unholy glee and engulfed her completely. The evil spirit used the winds to carry the maiden's body up and throw her over the ledge of the falls. Po-ho-no watched as the maiden plunged to her rocky death bed.

The older woman was terrified by what she saw unfold. She quickly made her way down the cliff, navigating the rough terrain as best she could. She ran back to the tribe's camp, crying out that Po-ho-no, "the Spirit of the Evil Wind," had drawn the maiden in.

After hearing the old woman's story, the old chief of Ah-wah-nee warned all other members of his tribe to never venture into the mists of Po-ho-no. He warned them it was the abode of an evil spirit that would draw them in and throw them over the falls to their deaths, where their spirits would be carried down into Po-ho-no's land of darkness and misery, to be held captive unless Po-ho-no secured another victim. To this day, it is told that another Ah-wah-nee has never ventured into the grips of Po-ho-no since the maiden's death, though the spirit continues to haunt Bridalveil Fall.

CHAPTER THREE

HAUNTED YOSEMITE

The Haunting of the Ahwahnee Hotel

The Ahwahnee Hotel in Yosemite National Park was opened in 1927 and is one of the United States' most distinctive Registered National Landmarks. The Ahwahnee offers every comfort needed, right in the hub of the Sierra Mountain terrain. There are also some potentially unwanted and uncomfortable amenities included. There are believed to be two World War II-era ghosts that haunt the mezzanine level of the hotel, which could be due to the fact that the Ahwahnee Hotel was also used as a naval convalescent hospital during the war. Numerous other spirits are said to inhabit the hotel, including Mary Curry Tressider, who took part in the hotel's design and opening, and none other than President John F. Kennedy.

After Mary Curry Tressider aided in the design, she actually lived in a private apartment at the Ahwahnee Hotel until her death in 1970, and it is believed to be her spirit that began haunting guests on the sixth floor shortly thereafter. Since then, sightings of her ghost are frequently reported by the hotel guests and personnel. Her spirit is said to be more of a prankster than a threatening entity, as she is known for performing nurturing actions like tucking in guests as they sleep or folding their clothes that were previously strewn about. Guests have also reported having their items moved around their rooms, and being called out to by Mary's ghost.

US President John F. Kennedy stayed on the third floor of the Ahwahnee Hotel during a visit to Yosemite in 1962. During his stay, a rocking chair was placed in the room at the president's own request, as he had complained of his constant and well-known back pain. Kennedy reportedly spent plenty of time in the chair, rocking away the time and back pain, perhaps contemplating his future, without knowing the darkness that truly lay ahead.

After his visit was over and he vacated the premises, the chair was removed from the hotel room. However, seemingly immediately after his tragic death by assassination in 1963, there are often reports of a spectral rocking chair mysteriously appearing in the room where the president slept. The chair has even been seen moving by itself about the halls and other rooms of the third floor.

Various other occurrences are reported in the hotel, including the sightings of apparitions and the hearing of disembodied footsteps. It's as if the Ahwahnee Hotel, or perhaps the majestic land of Yosemite, or maybe a sinister resident holds on to some visitors for good...

CHAPTER FOUR

UNEXPLAINED DISAPPEARANCES FROM YOSEMITE NATIONAL PARK

Emerson Holt

Fifty-five-year-old Emerson Holt disappeared on July 18, 1943, more than seventy-five years ago now, while hiking at Yosemite National Park.

Emerson was vice president of the Riverside Title Company and was well-known to many villagers. A large search party was assembled shortly after he disappeared, but nothing was found.

An article in the *San Bernardino Sun*, published July 24, 1943, states that Yosemite National Park officials described Emerson's disappearance as "mystifying." Emerson was with a large group of friends when he went missing. They left Happy Isles, heading for Lake Camp, which was seven miles away. When the group was almost to their destination, Emerson reportedly complained of a pain in his legs and had to sit and rest. He told the group that he would catch up, but they never saw him again.

Emerson frequented the trails at Yosemite and was no stranger to its terrain. Even so, the area he went missing in wasn't nearly as dangerous as some other areas of the park.

The park superintendent at the time, Frank Kittredge, said the group were alarmed when Emerson didn't return, and the search began immediately. He also said that he and other park officials were puzzled because the Merced River where Emerson rested is shallow and not swift, and there were no cliffs or deep pools of water for several hundred yards. How did Emerson disappear without a trace so close to his destination, with so many people around?

On August 6, 1943, the search was getting more intense and was still well underway, as reported by the *Desert Sun Newspaper*. No later digitized articles were found on Emerson Holt's disappearance, and his ultimate fate remains unknown. He would be 132 years old if he were alive today. As of February 3, 2021, Emerson's case remains unsolved, and there have been no further updates.

Louis A. Miller

Seventy-three-year-old Louis Miller disappeared in September of 1950, from somewhere in the vicinity of the Mono Pass Trail, south of Tioga Pass, at the end of the old road.

In *Guardians of the Yosemite*, Ranger John recalled that he was at Tuolumne Meadow Ranger Station the day Louis went missing.

Louis and his son, L. R. Miller, were fishing that day, and they had temporarily separated to fish independently. Louis was going up Dana Fork, while his son, L. R., fished downstream. They were supposed to meet back at the car around 5 p.m., but Louis never showed up. His son quickly alerted authorities.

Ranger John wrote about Louis' search and rescue:

"I organized a ranger search team immediately made up of Ranger Lowery Brown and another ranger, and two members of the Miller family. We searched along the stream with lanterns until midnight with no success. Early next morning we got additional help from headquarters. Thirty searchers spent all day without finding a trace... We had searchers out in the area for ten days without success. Mounted rangers combed the area... but found nothing. Notices were posted on the east side of the Sierra at various points with the hope that if he was a victim of amnesia or made his way out on foot someone would recognize him walking along a trail or road. [Louis] disappeared without a trace and what happened to him has remained a complete mystery to this day. Anyone with information concerning the missing man should contact his son, L. R. Miller, at 917 14th Street, Antioch, California."

As of this writing in mid-2021, Louis' case remains unsolved, and there have been no further updates.

Walter A. Gordon

Twenty-six-year-old Walter Gordon disappeared on July 20, 1954, while he was believed to be hiking up the Ledge Trail to Glacier Point.

Walter was a University of California researcher, a Yosemite park employee, and an overall experienced hiker. Walter was carrying a boxed lunch and planned to stop and eat somewhere along Ledge Trail.

Former Yosemite Park ranger John W. Bingaman recounted Walter's disappearance, along with many others, in Chapter 7 of his 1961 publication *Guardians of the Yosemite*.

Ranger John writes that Walter was working at Camp Curry in Yosemite, and when he was reported missing, the other rangers went out looking. He said regarding the search-and-rescue operation: "Rangers searched for many days... bloodhounds and a helicopter were used, but no trace of him was ever found."

The helicopter used in the search for Walter was one of the first used in the park.

Despite the extensive efforts, nothing was found. How did a young, agile employee of the park disappear on a hike that he likely would have taken many times before? As of February 3, 2021, Walter's case remains unsolved, and there have been no further updates.

———

Orvar Laass

Thirty-year-old Orvar Laass disappeared on October 9, 1954 (not quite three months after Walter Gordon went missing), while on a hike in the vicinity of Sugar Pine Bridge in Yosemite Valley.

Orvar was from Berkeley, California, and was visiting with his family in the Yosemite area at the time of his disappearance.

Former park ranger John Bingaman wrote about Orvar's case in *Guardians of the Yosemite* and said, "He disappeared completely and was never found although rangers searched for days."

Ranger John also wrote in his publication about both Orvar and Walter (the previous case) saying, "The case [*sic*] of Gordon and Laass were very strange for there were no clues as to what happened to them."

As of the time of this writing in 2021, Orvar's case remains unsolved, and there have been no further updates.

Tom Opperman

Twenty-one-year-old Tom Opperman disappeared on August 8, 1967. Tom's last known location was Merced Lake. He was heading out to hike Clark Mountain in Yosemite.

Tom's plan was to hike Mount Clark, then head to Glacier Point and return to the valley two days later on August 10.

An extensive search was undertaken when Tom was reported missing, and sometime during the search, sixteen US Marines were brought in to help. After a week, the main search was scaled back to cover only the Merced Lake and Clark Mountain areas.

The assistant park superintendent at the time, David

Condon, said after the week-long extensive search, "We feel the young man probably met up with some misfortune."

On September 25, 1967, a three-man team set out on what would be the last searching attempt at locating Tom. Nothing was discovered on this final search attempt.

As of this writing in mid-2021, Tom's case remains unsolved, and there have been no further updates.

Jane Doe

This case has a slightly different set of circumstances than a normal missing persons case. The disappearance was near Yosemite, and the missing person case that correlates with Jane Doe, if one exists, has not been discovered, so her identity remains unknown.

Seventeen-to-thirty-year-old Jane Doe's partial remains were discovered in Yosemite's Summit Meadow along Glacier Point Road in 1983.

Jane Doe's cause of death was human foul play, and the suspect in this case was Henry Lee Lucas, who was interviewed by authorities in 1980 and eventually died in prison in 2001. He knew facts about Jane Doe's case that were never revealed to the public and could only be known by the guilty party, so it is reasonable to believe that he was responsible for her death.

Jane Doe's identity remains unknown despite any information given by Henry Lucas before his death. He stated that in the early 1980s, he had picked up a female hitchhiker on Highway 41 somewhere between Fresno, California, and Yosemite National Park. He said she was five feet five or five feet six and weighed approximately 100 to 125 lbs. She had long straight hair that was light brown to blond, and wore silver rings on both her hands.

Jane Doe is believed by forensic experts to have been at least in her late teens, though she could have been up to thirty years old. The National Park Service Investigative Services Branch has had special agents working with multiple labs and agencies to identify Jane Doe and bring closure to her family. A digital facial reconstruction was created by forensic artists using an anthropology exam along with a CT scan of the remains. (Click the link in the show notes corresponding with Jane Doe to read about the case and for a closer look at her facial reconstruction image, about three-quarters of the way down the page.)

If you have any information that you think could help the case and ultimately help identify Jane Doe, you are urged to call the National Park Service tip line at 888-653-0009.

These mysterious and unexplained disappearances have been happening probably for millennia, and they continue to happen daily, with our national parks being hot spots for these missing persons cases. It is recommended that everyone who plans on being within our national parks or out in the wilderness in general carry a personal locator beacon at all times, which transmits a distress signal with its location when activated, in the event that something goes wrong. While there could be any number of things or combination of things to blame for these cases, one thing is certain: something had to happen. Whether these people suffered some natural tragedy or disappeared through supernatural means, they did not simply vanish, though the official records would appear to be just that—vanishings. What do you think happened?

PART 2
JOSHUA TREE

Joshua Tree National Park is an American national park in southeastern California, east of Los Angeles and near Palm Springs. It is named after the Joshua trees (*Yucca brevifolia*) native to the Mojave Desert. Originally declared a national monument in 1936, Joshua Tree was redesignated as a national park in 1994 when the United States Congress passed the California Desert Protection Act. Encompassing a total of 790,636 acres (1,235.4 square miles; 3,199.6 square kilometers)—slightly larger than the state of Rhode Island—the park includes 429,690 acres (671.4 square miles; 1,738.9 square kilometers) of designated wilderness. Straddling San Bernardino and Riverside Counties, the park includes parts of two deserts, each an ecosystem whose characteristics are determined primarily by elevation:

the higher Mojave Desert and the lower Colorado Desert. The Little San Bernardino Mountains traverse the southwest edge of the park.

The earliest known residents of the land in and around what later became Joshua Tree National Park were the people of the Pinto Culture, who lived and hunted here between 8000 and 4000 BCE. Their stone tools and spear points, discovered in the Pinto Basin in the 1930s, suggest that they hunted game and gathered seasonal plants, but little else is known about them. Later residents included the Serrano, the Cahuilla, and the Chemehuevi peoples. All three lived at times in small villages in or near water, particularly the Oasis of Mara in what non-aboriginals later called Twentynine Palms. They were hunter-gatherers who subsisted largely on plant foods supplemented by small game, amphibians, and reptiles while using other plants for making medicines, bows and arrows, baskets, and other articles of daily life. A fourth group, the Mojaves, used the local resources as they traveled along trails between the Colorado River and the Pacific coast. In the twenty-first century, small numbers of all four peoples live in the region near the park; the Twentynine Palms Band of Mission Indians, descendants of the Chemehuevi, own a reservation in Twentynine Palms.

In 1772, a group of Spaniards led by Pedro Fages

made the first European sightings of Joshua trees while pursuing native converts to Christianity who had run away from a mission in San Diego. By 1823, the year Mexico achieved independence from Spain, a Mexican expedition from Los Angeles, in what was then Alta California, is thought to have explored as far east as the Eagle Mountains in what later became the park. Three years later, Jedediah Smith led a group of American fur trappers and explorers along the nearby Mojave Trail, and others soon followed. Two decades after that, the United States defeated Mexico in the Mexican-American War (1846–48) and took over about half of Mexico's original territory, including California and the future parkland.

CHAPTER FIVE

BILL MELDER'S JOSHUA TREE ENCOUNTER

It all started on the last week of December in 2012. My mother and I were relaxing after work, watching TV, when out of the corner of my eye, I noticed movement in our hallway. When I turned to look, I noticed two shadowy-like figures that appeared on our hallway wall. In disbelief of what I was seeing—I turned my head over towards my mother, and right as I did, she made eye contact with me and simply said: "You see them, don't you?" I said yes. She told me not to acknowledge them because they are entities that can sense fear. But in disbelief—I looked back over at the hallway wall, and they were gone.

A few days had gone by, and my mother told me she felt a sense of dread... And said someone in our family was going to pass away before the end of the year.

Well, on New Year's Eve 2012, my mother and I celebrated at home. We watched the movie *Tron* and had a pizza delivered to ring in the new year. I've always been a real mama's boy, so this was an ideal way for me to spend my New Year's.

Around 11 p.m. that night we saw the two figures again—this time we both experienced an overwhelming quietness and sense of urgency and dread... We both did our best to ignore it, and eventually the shadowy figures and the senses went away. We discussed the experience, and again my mother told me to never acknowledge "them," and before I could press her for more details, my mother started telling me how much I meant to her and that I would go on to do good things in my life... She loved me... etc.... She then got up and walked towards the kitchen, turned around and said, "I love you," then fell to the ground.

I had previous EMT training and am certified in CPR, so I called 911 and explained to them my mother was in cardiac arrest and I needed medical assistance ASAP! I was doing CPR on my mother for nearly twenty minutes, and for anyone who has ever done CPR —it is not easy! The EMTs arrived at 11:38 p.m., and my mother was taken to the emergency room. By this time our neighbor and friend Bonnie had rushed over to my house and drove me to the hospital.

When I checked in at the front desk, I was taken to a small private room, and the head physician told me that my mother had passed away. The autopsy showed my mother suffered from a fatal heart attack, and her time of death was 11:59 p.m. on December 31, 2012. When I was taken in to see her one last time, her lips were blue, she was cool to the touch, but she was still my mom... So I just hugged her and couldn't let go for nearly thirty minutes. Thankfully my neighbor Bonnie was there and gave me plenty of support and encouragement to leave, as my mother would want me to stay strong.

Fast-forward a about six months after my mother died—I had quit my job and had become a recluse. I would only leave my house to purchase groceries. I quickly realized how severely depressed I was and decided it was time to get away. I ended up traveling to Joshua Tree National Park and decided it would be my getaway to find some peace and closure. I left the second or third week in June. I notified my neighbor Bonnie not to worry, that I was just going on a day's hike and I would be back by midnight.

When I arrived at Joshua Tree, I parked my Jeep and entered the Lost Palms Oasis Trail... After a few hours of walking/hiking, I stopped to take a break and eat. As I finished up and looked around, nothing looked familiar, and I in fact was not on any trail. I was not too worried and felt confident I would find my way back.

But as I made my way through the desert landscape that I did not recall ever passing, I started feeling like I was being watched. I started to panic. Then I started hearing strange growling noises... But could not determine from what direction they were coming from... It almost seemed they were all around me. So I stood in one spot and made a 360-degree rotation, and as I came to a stop, I saw something transparent—no defining shape—just a blur directly in front of me that was coming closer and closer to where I was standing. I quickly turned around and started walking faster and faster in the opposite direction and then experienced the same overwhelming quietness and sense of urgency and dread I had experienced with my mother just six months prior.

Then all of the sudden almost like a snap of a finger, daytime turned into night. I wasn't sure what was going on but knew something wasn't right. After walking around in the dark—I found myself by a large rock (about as big as a large SUV) and felt safest there. I put my back against the rock; this way I felt nothing would sneak up behind me. I used the night to hydrate and eat some snacks I'd brought. I remember trying to make sense out of what I was experiencing, but knew that my mother and I had already experienced something within our own home... but at least when I was home, I felt safe! Here I was vulnerable and alone.

As I tried to rest that night, I started seeing a number of shadowy entities walking around in the desert... Almost as if they were wandering around aimlessly... It freaked me out! And the more I acknowledged "them," the closer they got to me. At one time during that night, I remember feeling something breathing down my neck (remember my back was against a huge rock)... I just closed my eyes and did my best to keep them shut. The last thing I remember about that night was opening my eyes and seeing three shadowy figures (one at each side and one directly in front of me).

Then once again in a snap it was morning. I would experience this same weirdness for two more days until the last day. On the last day of me roaming around Joshua Tree, I hadn't had any food or water since the initial first night. I was scared and dehydrated. I came upon another large rock and remembered in my EMT training that digging a hole near a rock in the desert will keep you cool and less likely to get severe sunburn. I did just that and thought to myself, *I am literally digging my own grave.* By the time I lay down in the two-foot arched hole I had made, covered my chest and legs up with dirt, I blacked out. I don't remember anything for the rest of that day or night.

The next morning I was woken up by an off-duty search and rescue employee who was literally making me choke on water... I remember him saying, "there are a whole lot of people out looking for you, buddy." I was picked up by helicopter and taken to Regional Medical Center in Palm Springs, California. In the days during my recovery, I saw two detectives, a number of psychiatrists, and my neighbor Bonnie was there at the hospital by my side 100% of the way.

The detectives wanted to close the missing persons report my neighbor Bonnie made the second day I was missing. But they asked me strange questions like, was I using a flare gun in the area?—no. Why had I purchased a large amount of camping gear and survival materials prior to my hike?—I was going for a hike. Strange questions to ask someone? Or maybe it's just me.

The physician stated I was going to kill myself due to the loss of my mother, but honestly that never crossed my mind. The psychiatrists told me I didn't experience anything but hallucinations due to lack of food and water/dehydration. My neighbor Bonnie overheard my story and later confided in me that she too experienced similar shadowy figures when she hiked in Joshua Tree.

When I arrived back home, she used sage and other

new age methods to rid my house of whatever darkness was there. However, it continued all the way up until my move to Tennessee in 2014. By far the most aggressive was the transparent entities that were in Joshua Tree. I felt like everything was about to end when I encountered them.

I've always wondered if my mother experienced more than what happened that night. I'm not sure what the hell happened those few days in Joshua Tree National Park, but from what I can remember: during the moments when daytime would turn into nighttime in a snap—I felt like I was falling down or being suspended in midair before completely realizing what was going on. I also remember a strong urge to go to Joshua Tree. I would think about going all the time, and when I finally went, I almost felt like I was "called" there by something.

My sister often talks about my first week living in Tennessee… She has said she felt like a demon was attached to me. One night as I slept on her couch, I woke up with her putting holy water on my head and saying a prayer over me. But I don't believe in all of that, I used to, but nowadays, I have an easier time believing in alien abductions and portals rather than being followed around by a demon. But then again, who knows, right?

Finally, I can tell you with 100% honesty, I experienced all of the above. I can't explain what it or what they were, but I can tell you I feel like my life was spared for some strange reason. Perhaps I did not meet the requirements for whatever it is that, "they" need. Looking back now, I never would have gone hiking alone... But again, I remember this irresistible urge to go to Joshua Tree and would frequently feel like I was called there.

CHAPTER SIX

BODIES, MURDER & DISAPPEARANCES IN
JOSHUA TREE

Perhaps the most famous body ever in Joshua Tree was that of a country rock musician, as we shall see later on, but that's a different story entirely. His body was purposely brought into Joshua Tree National Park for an impromptu open-air cremation by his friend and road manager (although he did die in the Joshua Tree Inn). But there are a lot of bodies that tend to show up in the area around Joshua Tree as a result of more evil and nefarious incidents.

A few years ago, after the four bodies of the McStay family were pulled from the ground, former deputy chief of San Bernardino County Sheriff's Department Keith Bushey said, "If there were to be a cross everywhere someone dumped a body, the desert would look like Forest Lawn."

In more recent times, at least two more corpses were dug up within Joshua Tree's boundaries within the space of a month. The first was skeletal remains, discovered in early May by hikers near Stubbe Springs Loop, a thirteen-mile trail over fairly difficult terrain. "It was all bones," says George Land, the park's public information officer. Forensic specialists investigated the scene, and the remains are now with the Riverside County Coroner's office until they can be identified. Land says he's waiting on DNA tests to come back and that there are a few open missing-person cases they think could match. At this point, they're working on the assumption that the death was accidental. That was certainly not the case with the second body.

A hiker discovered those remains near Big Horn Pass Road, partially buried about two feet down. "As the gases release and putrefaction sets in," Land says, "we have a number of scavengers out here, like coyotes and vultures, and they were digging at the lower half."

As Land points out, bodies don't bury themselves. So when rangers arrived on scene, they shut down the area while police investigated. The case is now in the hands of Riverside's Central Homicide Unit.

Two bodies in the span of a month is certainly abnormal, but it's not really all that shocking. The same qualities that have made the desert around Joshua Tree ideal for a weekend getaway—a combination of ease of access and remoteness—also make it a convenient place to dump a body. The entire Mojave Desert is about 50,000 square miles, and its defining geographic characteristics are the Joshua trees, of course, and its otherworldly desolation. It's a few hours from any major city, but three interstates connect it to metropolises like Los Angeles, Phoenix, and Las Vegas.

For a long time, the Mojave, though not specifically Joshua Tree, was the rumored cemetery for Vegas mobsters. (As Joe Pesci said in the mafia movie *Casino*, there are "a lot of holes in the desert, and a lot of problems are buried in those holes.") No corpses have been found in the Mojave rolled up in carpet recently (not since 2000 at least), but in 2014, a nineteen-year-old woman was strangled by her lover, and her body was found dumped at the bottom of an abandoned mine shaft just outside Joshua Tree. Last fall, a couple was found in a remote region of the park, dead beneath a Joshua tree and locked in what seemed to be a last loving embrace as they tried to cool themselves in the shade. It later turned out their deaths were a murder-suicide.

Of course, not all bodies end up in the desert through suspicious means. Like many parks these days, visitation in Joshua Tree is way up. More than three million people are expected to fight for its three thousand parking spots and wander the trails this year—double the visitors from five years ago. Some blame the recent boom on the nearby Coachella music festival and the social media–induced "loved to death" syndrome that's plaguing so many of our parks.

Irish rock band U2 certainly deserves some of the blame as well. Their 1987 seminal rock album, *The Joshua Tree*, is in particular the cause of some strange treks into the desert by misguided fans on some sort of pilgrimage. The tree photographed for the sleeve fell around 2000, yet the site remains a popular tourist attraction for U2 fans. One person inserted a plaque into the ground, reading "Have you found what you're looking for?" in reference to the album's track "I Still Haven't Found What I'm Looking For." It is a common misconception that the site is within Joshua Tree National Park, when in fact it is over two hundred miles away from the park.

While U2's album cover for *The Joshua Tree* was not shot inside the park, here are some pop culture moments that do involve the actual area in and around Joshua Tree:

In 1972, the album cover photos for *Eagles* were shot in Joshua Tree National Monument.

In 1973, Phil Kaufman cremated singer/songwriter Gram Parsons' remains in the park. A whole chapter dedicated to this as well as my own personal experiences can be found elsewhere in this section.

In 1994, American Tejano singer Selena recorded her music video for "Amor Prohibido" at Joshua Tree National Park.

In 2008, an episode of *Entourage* aired that featured Vince and the gang going to Joshua Tree and taking shrooms to figure out his next career move. This was the fifth episode of season 5 and aired on HBO.

The black comedy crime film *Seven Psychopaths* (2012) was partly filmed in the park, as were a whole slew of other film and television productions, mainly westerns, beginning with *Borderland* (1937), a Hopalong Cassidy feature.

In 2016, Donald Glover (or Childish Gambino) performed six sold-out shows in Joshua Tree in promotion of his new album, *Awaken, My Love!* The three-day event went by the name Pharos.

In 2017, American rock band Walk the Moon recorded the video "One Foot" in the park during that summer's solar eclipse.

Meanwhile, national park staffing in Joshua Tree has remained the same. About 110 paid employees watch over 1,200 square miles of land, some of the hottest in the United States, where it's easy to become lost in the famous red-stone mounds that give Joshua Tree its

Martian look. All those extra visitors mean more people who wander off the trail—and some of them die. In April, a seventy-six-year-old man named David Sewell was lost for three days. Rescuers miraculously found him by following the circling vultures overhead. When they spotted Sewell, he was on death's edge, covered in dirt and curled around a rock (see Bill Melder's remarkably similar story in Chapter Six).

Sewell was lucky. But as we've been made aware, about 1,600 other people who've gone missing on public land weren't so fortunate. The thing that sets Joshua Tree and the Mojave apart from all the other places where people disappear, however, is the stunning regularity at which their bodies resurface.

For many, the vast expanses of the Mojave Desert between Victorville and Las Vegas provide relaxing scenic views for those who drive to and from the Golden and Silver states.

But to some, the region has served a more sinister purpose—as a location to dispose of bodies or to commit murder.

The skeletal remains of four people, unearthed from two shallow graves on Wednesday in an off-roading area near Stoddard Wells Road, west of the 15 Freeway and just north of Victorville, left some pondering that darker side of the Mojave.

Keith Bushey, the former San Bernardino County sheriff's deputy chief and Los Angeles police commissioner who made the comment above about the desert looking like Forest Lawn if crosses were placed where bodies were found in the desert, also had this to say:

> "If you want to kill somebody, you're going to take him some place that's desolate, and the California desert is just a wonderful place and it's a secluded place. In addition to all the wonderful things it has to offer, it's long been a place to dump bodies."

Apple Valley resident Debra Andrews saw the sheriff's vehicles and news vans from the 15 Freeway on Wednesday afternoon and pulled off to see what was going on. She was shocked when she heard what investigators were unearthing.

"This is something you would hear about outside of Vegas or in the LA forest area. You don't find it up here very often," said Andrews.

She said she could definitely see the appeal of remote desert areas for killers looking for ideal places to dump bodies, dead by whatever means.

"It seems like you can bury anything out in the desert, and it's going to take a while for someone to find it. It's unfortunate," Andrews said. "You have so many unincorporated areas out here, you're bound to have bodies that are dumped. Until we can stop the crime, there's nothing we can really do about it."

THE REMOTE STRETCH of Mojave Desert between Victorville and Las Vegas has seen its share of murder victims, either dumped or killed on-site.

In one well-remembered crime in way back in February of 1978, Canoga Park teens Jacqueline Bradshaw, eighteen, and her brother Malcolm, seventeen, were abducted from a Barstow gas station and taken to an area of the desert east of the 15 Freeway near Hodge Road, about ten miles south of Barstow, and beaten to death. A sheepherder found their badly decomposed bodies about a month later.

In May of 2004, William Floyd Zamastil, a suspected serial killer, pleaded guilty to slaying the teens. Per a plea bargain, Zamastil was sentenced to twenty-five years to life in prison, to run concurrent with a twenty-five-year-to-life sentence he was already serving at a Wisconsin prison for the abduction, rape and murder of a woman there also in 1978 following the Bradshaw murders.

Zamastil was a creepy drifter type (shades of Henry Lee Lucas) believed to have trekked the Mojave Desert, from Needles to Barstow, all throughout the entire decade of the 1970s, leaving a trail of victims, mainly young men and women, in his path. Authorities suspect him of committing at least five additional homicides (and quite possibly a lot more) in not only California but in Arizona as well.

THE DESOLATE AREA north of Victorville is also well known as a hotbed of motorized off-road activity. Mainly outlaw motorcycles, but sometimes any wheeled conveyance with a motor (or motors) attached can be seen noisily and speedily tearing through the desert. On more than one occasion, it has been an off-road motorcyclist who came across the remains and notified deputies.

"It's ridden quite a bit by four- and two-wheelers," said Chris Hayes, a parts associate for Victorville Motorcycle Center. "It's a real rocky area, a lot of heavy brush. It's pretty popular. It's just a legal riding area for all off-roaders."

Hayes said that for a person to bury human remains "somebody's awful brave."

Shaun Merenda, the general manager of a motorcycle parts and repair shop called Action Motorsports in nearby Hesperia, said that portion of the desert is "one of the few areas still open to riding.

"It's nice and open. We don't have any other place to go."

Mickey Quillman, the chief of resources for the Barstow office of the US Bureau of Land Management, said the area was a "patchwork" of private and BLM land with designated routes in the area for riders.

"West of the 15, north of Stoddard there's a lot of private land," Quillman said. "And some BLM land. A lot of people like to shoot shotguns, which is legal on the BLM land, but you can't do it if it's privatized."

WHAT FOLLOWS ARE JUST a few of the stories of people who were found deceased under strange circumstances in and around the desert areas of Joshua Tree:

Erika Ashley Lloyd, disappeared on June 16 of 2020. Her body was found on January 31, 2021, in the area of Wonder Valley, California.

Erika Ashley Lloyd, thirty-seven years old, was a

single mother with a twelve-year-old son. On June 11, 2020, Erika dropped her son off with her ex and on June 14 told her family and friends she was going on a "pandemic road trip".

She set out on a five-hundred-mile, seven-hour trip from her home in Walnut Creek, heading to Joshua Tree National Park in California, a place that would routinely see temps above 100° Fahrenheit at that time of the year. Quite the road trip, indeed. At some point later on, her wrecked Honda Accord was discovered abandoned in the desert by the police near the intersection of Highway 62 and Shelton Road in the area of Twentynine Palms. Erika, however, was nowhere to be found. A preliminary search in the immediate area and the campground where she had been staying while in Joshua Tree failed to turn up any clues as to her whereabouts.

Sadly, yet somehow not surprisingly, Erika's remains were eventually discovered in January of 2021 and, oddly enough, preceded by the discovery of another two sets of unrelated remains in October 2020 in the general vicinity of where her car had been found. One of these sets of remains was later identified as a missing cyclist, James Escalante, who had vanished in the area in late June 2020 whilst searching for a friend of his girlfriend. His disappearance occurred within just a few days of that of Erika.

Is it mere coincidence that three cases of apparent murder happened so close together in the area near Twentynine Palms, or is there something more sinister and mysterious afoot? Many have described the area as having an "odd vibe," me among them. It's an unnamable something that just feels off about the whole area. We all know that the desert can be a very unforgiving and brutal place not only during the heat of midsummer, but almost any time of the year. However, these cases have more than a few quite strange and very disturbing elements to them. Can this really be chalked up to mental illness, death by simple misadventure, or is there truly something evil out there in the sand?

WILLIAM "BILL" Michael Ewasko disappeared on the 24th of June 2010 from Joshua Tree National Park, California.

Bill Ewasko, sixty-six, was last spotted in Riverside County, California, on June 24, 2010, after leaving his home in Marietta, Georgia, (a suburb in the greater Atlanta area) where he lived with his girlfriend. Bill, vacationing in the area, was planning a solo hiking trip in Joshua Tree National Park that day and had packed a light lunch, bottled water and energy snacks for his excursion. He was supposed to have finished his hike and returned to his vehicle so that he could call his girlfriend at 5:00 p.m., but the call was never made. His girlfriend contacted the authorities at Joshua Tree National Park and reported him missing the very next day, around 8 a.m. in the Pacific time zone.

The white 2007 Chrysler Sebring with the California license plate number 6CVF834, which Bill had rented, was found in a parking area on Keys View Road. Despite an extensive search, no sign of Bill was to be found. At the time he went missing, temperatures in the park that week reached very near to 100° Fahrenheit (38°C).

Other than a bandana thought to have belonged to Bill, nothing has ever been found despite many man-hours of both official and unofficial searches.

Bill Ewasko was a military vet, having served in Vietnam. He was also considered to be a knowledgeable and experienced hiker who had made the trip to Joshua Tree National Park on several occasions previously. At the time of his disappearance in 2010, he was in good physical shape and had no known medical issues. Bill was also known as an avid jogger and a lover of nature and the great outdoors in general.

Bill had flown into LAX airport in Los Angeles on Wednesday, June 23, 2010, for what would (unbeknownst to him) be his last trip to Joshua Tree National Park. He spent the night in the greater Los Angeles area at a friend's vacant condo before making the drive to Joshua Tree early on the morning of the following day, June 24. Bill planned to spend a week in the area and then catch a return flight home on July 1, and had another trip, this time to Florida, planned on his return.

On his way into the park the morning of June 24, Bill made two cell phone calls, reporting that he was on Interstate 10 near Palm Desert, a location that authorities were able to verify by cell phone records. The first call was to his friend, the owner of the condominium where Bill had spent the night. Bill had called to offer thanks for being able to stay.

The second call Bill made was to his girlfriend, Mary Winston. He'd left behind a rough itinerary for her prior to leaving Georgia, which featured multiple destinations, both inside and outside the park. His first hike, on Thursday, June 24, was meant to be a loop out and back from a remote historic site known as Carey's Castle, an old miner's hut built into the rocks. Carey's Castle is so archaeologically fragile that, to discourage visitors, the National Park Service does not include it on official maps, and it is very isolated and remote. Certainly off the beaten track.

During his call to Mary that morning, she said that

he was in high spirits in anticipation of the day, although she was somewhat concerned about the relative dangers of him visiting such a desolate and isolated location. Mary said that she even tried gently to persuade him to go hiking somewhere else. However, Bill did not offer to change his plans. He did promise Mary that he expected to be out of the park by 5 p.m. Pacific time and had plans to take his dinner in nearby Pioneertown at a restaurant called Pappy and Harriet's, where he'd eaten at on previous trips to the area. He reassured Mary that he would call and let her know he was okay as soon as he was out of the national park.

However, 5 p.m. came and went with Mary receiving no phone call from Bill. She tried calling his cell phone several different times, but it continually went to voicemail. Mary thought that perhaps Bill might still be in an area with poor cell phone reception. Later that evening, Mary became even more worried that Bill hadn't called, so she tried to call someone at the national park, but by that time the administrative offices at Joshua Tree headquarters had already closed for the day.

The next morning at around 8 a.m. Pacific time, Mary finally got through to Joshua Tree park rangers and reported that Bill seemed to have gone missing in the area around Carey's Castle. The park rangers duly noted Mary's concerns and headed over to the trailhead to have a look around. However, when they arrived, the Chrysler Sebring Bill had rented was nowhere to be found. According to the park rangers, the trail appeared to not have been visited by Bill, and looked as if it had not had any visitors in some time. For whatever purpose, it appeared that Bill had veered from his loose itinerary and had changed his plans for some reason unknown.

Joshua Tree National Park's deputy planning chief, Dave Pylman (also a former executive director of Friends of Joshua Tree, a climbing-advocacy group, as well as a nineteen-year veteran of Joshua Tree Search and Rescue), was tapped to be in charge of assigning routes, teams and search areas. Dave said that at first thought, he assumed Bill was just the typical lost tourist, which the parks sees plenty of: someone who goes out by themselves, encounters a difficulty of some sort, or gets temporarily lost and fails to report back at a prearranged time or place, but manages to eventually find their way back to where they were headed. It's not unusual for Joshua Tree to see perhaps as many as fifty cases such as this every year. Learning that Bill was a healthy, experienced hiker added to Dave Pylman's confidence that he would be found quickly and perhaps even experience a "self-rescue" by finding his own way out of wherever he had gone to. "The thing I remember the most," Pylman said, "was the frustration of: How can this be? How can we have so much information about where he was going to go, or at least where he said he was going to go—why can't we find him?"

Carey's Castle was only one of several locations Bill had listed on his possible itinerary. Unfortunately, the list included sites as far-flung as places such as the Salton Sea and Mount San Jacinto, each one more than an hour's drive from Joshua Tree National Park. Other trails inside Joshua Tree were also listed as possibilities on the list he'd given Mary. There was an overlook with views of the San Andreas Fault known as Keys View, as well as the Joshua Tree's highest point, the exposed summit of Quail Mountain. Literally, Bill could be anywhere within a couple of hours' drive in any particular direction. One can imagine how frustrating and confusing this was for the search and rescue teams. It would be like finding the proverbial needle in a haystack with what they currently had to go on.

Strangely enough, the park rangers quickly established that Bill's national parks pass had never been scanned at either park entrance at Joshua. Now, that's not necessarily definitive proof of anything. As can sometimes happen, if a long line of cars forms to enter the park, rangers will sometimes just wave pass holders through, but the concerning part of this is that it meant that there was absolutely no record of Bill having visited

Joshua Tree. The park rangers had to take this odd fact into account and wonder if Bill had even entered Joshua Tree National Park at all.

That next Saturday, the 26th of June, it had been nearly two full days since Bill Ewasko had failed to show up. A Los Angeles County sheriff's deputy was sent to the friend's still empty borrowed condominium where Bill had spent the night to search for additional clues. The deputy found maps and additional itineraries. On one of the left-behind itineraries Bill had written the following for the day he had disappeared: "Thousand Palms, Joshua Tree all day, Lost Horse Mountain." Unfortunately, this added little to almost no information to what was already known. It was just too similar to the information the authorities already had at their disposal.

However, later that Saturday, a California Highway Patrol helicopter finally spotted Bill's rental car. It had been left at the Juniper Flats trailhead, which is almost a full ninety-minute drive from the Carey's Castle trailhead where they thought he'd been. At this juncture in time, the authorities reasoned, Bill would have been exposed to the moderately severe outdoor elements (late June temperatures in the mid-90s, and little or no food or water), which made the prognosis for survival slim at best. However, finding the car did confirm that Bill, indeed, had been inside Joshua Tree National Park. It was decided that the searchers redeploy to the Juniper Flats area, and it was also decided for other areas to be searched, particularly to the south around Keys View and near the summit of Quail Mountain, both places Bill had listed on his itinerary.

Having received confirmation around 7 p.m. that evening from the California Highway Patrol helicopter pilot that the license plate matched Bill's rental car, Joshua Tree National Park ranger Jimmy Pritchett was the first to arrive on the scene at the trailhead parking area. He examined Bill's rental car, but found no additional evidence. On the passenger seat of the car was a list of directions from the west entrance of the national park to Juniper Flats. Ranger Pritchett also observed footprints, which he felt seem to be very fresh.

Soon, Ranger Pritchett was joined by another park ranger and also the pilot from the CHP helicopter. Ranger Pritchett drove his work vehicle up the Juniper Flats Road, which is an old park service jeep trail. It's been closed to the public for a long time, but is often used by hikers as a shortcut to get to Quail Mountain. Ranger Pritchett had a portable bullhorn with him and repeatedly called out to Bill as he slowly drove up the dirt service road. No Bill. His calls had only been met with silence. Ranger Pritchett then returned to the trailhead parking area, where he and the others were shortly joined by deputies from the neighboring county as well as a group of trained search volunteers. Pritchett divided the group up into two teams of searchers and sent them to cover the California Riding and Hiking Trail (it runs roughly parallel to Juniper Flats Road and recrosses it near Juniper Flat), and Stubbe Springs Trail, a side loop trail. As the sun was beginning to set and the daylight was starting to fade fast, the two teams were only able to cover part of their assigned areas before suspending search and rescue efforts for the night.

When the teams returned to the trailhead lot, several of the searchers pointed out a nearby ridge and claimed that they had observed some kind of lights in the area. Ranger Pritchett took a look, but could not confirm that there were any lights or activity on the nearby ridge.

It was decided that a park ranger be left at the car overnight, just in case Bill were to appear. However, the next morning, when Bill still hadn't shown up, the search began again in earnest, with teams of both trained search and rescue volunteers as well as park personnel convening at around 7:30 a.m.

The teams spread out from the vicinity of Bill's rental car and started moving in the most likely areas where he might have ventured. The story about lights being seen along the nearby ridgeline the previous night was repeated and the area thoroughly searched, but absolutely nothing was to be found. However, a little later that morning, searchers found a red bandana on a ridge near Quail Mountain. They had no proof that it had even belonged to Bill, but it had obviously only been dropped very recently, and the authorities assumed it might be his. This lone bandana would be the only possible sign of Bill to be found during the whole search and rescue effort, and they couldn't even be sure about that.

By now, volunteer searchers were arriving from all across Southern California and beyond. An "incident command post" was established at Cap Rock to ease in communication to and deployment of teams of search and rescue volunteers. As helicopters whirred loudly overhead, searching a grid pattern from the air, scent dogs were given clothing of Bill's that had been found in the rental car and sent onto the trail. Still, Bill remained missing despite all the efforts.

The Riverside County Sheriff's Department was now actively assisting in the search, with more searchers on foot as well as some on horseback being deployed. One of the tracking dogs indicated that Bill may have taken the California Riding and Hiking Trail up to the point where it intersects with Juniper Flats Road around the area where it heads toward Quail Mountain, but then promptly lost the scent and was unable to track further. As this is a complex junction of all the trails in the immediate area, it really offered no real guidance as to which direction Bill might have gone afterwards.

That night, it was revealed that the previous morning, at about 6:30 a.m. or so, Bill's phone had pinged off a cell tower in the Yucca Valley area, a small town about twenty miles or so northwest of where his rental car had been found. This served to raise the hopes of the search crews that perhaps Bill was still alive and had been very lost and disoriented. Park rangers requisitioned a night helicopter with thermal-imaging capability to search the area, but to no avail. Still no sign of Bill.

On the following Tuesday, two water bottles hidden under a log were discovered within the search area. One of the scent dogs indicated a very high probability that both the bottles and the bandana were Bill's. Sadly, another hiker would come forward a bit later and claim that he'd been the one to stash the water bottles, which also cast doubt on the bandana belonging to Bill as well.

The only known visitor to Juniper Flats Trailhead the day Bill disappeared was a lone hiker named Greg Mendoza. Mendoza gave the time of his arrival in the park at around 10:20 a.m., and he said that at that time there were no other vehicles at the trailhead lot. He did state, however, that upon his return to the parking area at the trailhead between 5:30 and 6:00 p.m., he observed

Bill's rented Chrysler Sebring parked parallel and next to the curb on the north side of the parking area, rather than one of the diagonal designated parking spots. Greg also said that he saw a single line of fresh boot tracks heading up the old Juniper Flats road.

This fact means that Bill's car would have arrived at the trailhead parking lot no earlier than 10:20 a.m., leaving at a minimum a roughly two-and-a-half-hour gap from his last phone call to his arrival in the lot. Under normal circumstances, it should have only taken Bill about half that time to reach Juniper Flats trailhead, so it's not known where Bill could have been for the unaccounted extra hour or so.

Sadly, on July 5, 2010, the official search was called off. Bill had been missing for eleven days, and search and rescue effort funds had run out. It is presumed that without food and water and taking into account the extremes of the desert climate, Bill would not have been able to survive the ordeal.

But after the official search ended, the unofficial search continued, including Tom Mahood, a former search and rescue worker based in California. He is responsible for the discovery of the Death Valley Germans (Egbert Rimkus, Georg Weber, Cornelia Meyer, Max Meyer). After more than a year of hiking in the Death Valley area, on November 12, 2009, Mahood and another searcher found the remains of the German family who had disappeared in Death Valley thirteen years earlier on the 23rd of July 1996. Tom's website is located at https://www.otherhand.org. As of this writing in May, 2021, Tom has been unable to locate any sign of Bill Ewasko or his remains.

THE STRANGE DISAPPEARANCE of Laura Bradbury

On October 18, 1984, a three-and-a-half-year-old little girl named Laura Bradbury was on a camping trip with her family at the Indian Cove Campground in the Joshua Tree National Park, California.

Her parents, Patty and Michael, were regular visitors to the park. They were a family of five, who lived their day-to-day lives cramped in a two-bedroom condo, so a trip to the great outdoors of Joshua Tree offered a much-needed break and some precious space.

Laura and her eight-year-old brother, Travis, had gone to the portable restrooms located at the campground. Laura stayed outside while Travis used the toilet, but when he finished his business and came out, Laura had vanished.

Over 250 people along with horseback riders, scent dogs and CHP helicopters searched for Laura in the

Joshua Tree National Park and surrounding areas. The scent dogs were able to follow her scent for about two miles before losing it. Only three days after Laura disappeared, the official search was called off.

At this point, the Bradbury family decided to mobilize their own massive private search effort, convinced that Laura was alive and could still be found. They handed out literally millions of flyers and thousands of T-shirts with Laura's image and info on them. They also appeared on as many TV and radio talk shows as they could, and the disappearance was re-enacted twice on national TV network channels. A hotline was set up in order to hopefully receive tips and answer questions. The search for little Laura became a national story, and she was one of the first missing children to be featured on milk cartons, which was a new attempt at helping locate the missing at that time.

Witnesses came forward and claimed to have seen a man in his fifties driving a metallic blue van at Indian Cove Campground just a few minutes before Laura disappeared, and a man described as looking similar to the man at Indian Cove was also reported to have been near the Burns Canyon area just a few hours later on. The sheriff's department even brought in a certified hypnotist to try to help campers who had seen the fat bearded man and his van recall as many small details as possible.

Initially, the San Bernardino County Sheriff's Department had helmed the investigation into Laura's disappearance, but Mike Bradbury, Laura's father, had lost faith in the deputies and had decided that he and his family would put together their own search. Mike and the rest of Laura's family grew increasingly aggravated with what they considered the sheriff's deputies' poor handling of the case, as well as for not doing enough about the many tips that flowed into the Incident Command Center that had been set up for Laura's disappearance. Mike even went on record with his displeasure, telling news reporters that they deputies were either incompetent, lazy or both. He even hinted that someone inside the sheriff's department had intimate, secret knowledge and was covering up the fact that they knew that a kidnapper was involved.

Mike was particularly upset when he heard the rumor that Clifford Leville and Toby Santangelo were said to have given the deputies very reliable info concerning a man that they believed to be Laura's kidnapper. However, investigators allegedly checked it out and found it to not be credible. Strangely enough, not long after sharing the story with the law enforcement officials, both Leville and Santangelo were found mysteriously shot to death.

Mike, along with a private investigator he'd hired, continued to comb the isolated communities near Joshua Tree, where known drug dealers and other assorted oddballs liked to hang out. This endeavor, too, failed to turn up any credible evidence or worthy leads.

In 1986, almost two years after Laura's disappearance, a skull believed to belong to her was found by some hikers close to the park's west entrance, which was a couple of miles or so from where the family had been camping. However, DNA tests were inconclusive in proving that the skull was Laura's, as at that time they were not even able to identify blood type or gender. The only certainty was that the skull was that of a child.

A captain from the sheriff's department publicly speculated that he believed it was Laura's skull, and furthermore had a theory of how she met her demise. Maybe, he said, she wandered away from the toilet, stumbled and was somehow buried by collapsing sand. Only recently, some scavenging animal such as a coyote or a mountain lion had dug up all that was left of the remains.

Then, later in 1990, new and better DNA analysis methods were said to have proven the skull was indeed

Laura's, with the 99 percent likelihood of a positive match.

Sadly, Laura's mother, Patty, died in 2001, and her father, Michael, wrote a book in 2010 about his ordeal with his daughter's disappearance titled *Laura Ann Bradbury: A Father's Search*.

Since October 2009, Michael Bradbury has tried to have the skull transferred from the coroner's facility to a mortuary, but because the San Bernardino County coroner's office has not issued a death certificate, he was unable to claim his daughter's remains.

In a 2010 interview, he said he was shown about forty color 35 mm slides of the skull and was astonished to find out it is a full-sized skull, about seven inches by five inches, missing the teeth and lower jaw. He claimed that investigators showed him a completely different skull shortly after hikers discovered the remains. "My wife and I were shown a smaller, three-inch skullcap in or around 1986–87 that the sheriff's claimed was Laura's skull," he said. "The two skulls are totally dissimilar; they looked nothing like each other. I wonder now, what or whose skull they showed me then. And why?"

He also had a report on tests that provided inconclusive results on whether the cranium was his daughter's. According to the report, only one of four DNA tests performed on the skull matched DNA samples from

Laura's mother's blood. Even hair taken from Laura's hairbrush did not match DNA with the skull, he said. The two partial skull bones are the only remains Michael was aware of that are believed to be from his daughter. "I am very eager to put closure to this terrible period of my life," Bradbury said. "All I want is justice for my daughter. That's all I care about."

As of this writing in May, 2021, no arrests have ever been made, and the case remains unsolved.

The Disappearance of Paul Miller

In July 2018, Paul Miller, fifty-one, and his wife, Stephanie, from Ontario in Canada, were on vacation in California and Nevada and were planning to head to Las Vegas to celebrate their twenty-sixth wedding anniversary.

A typical vacation for them was camping in the backwoods, hiking and kayaking, and they had hiked across Canada, North America and Mexico. Both Paul and Stephanie were avid hikers who were in great shape and who loved exploring the outdoors.

On July 13, 2018, Paul decided he wanted to take one more short hike and headed for the 49 Palms Oasis Trail in Joshua Tree National Park. He promised

Stephanie he would be back later that morning. He was never seen again.

At the end of 2019, Paul's remains were discovered in Joshua Tree, in an area well off-trail, following analysis of drone footage. What happened to Paul Miller on his solo hike?

Paul Miller had a degree in environmental sciences and was working for a small company making water-filtration systems to bring water to different communities.

He was described by friends as being fun to be around, with lots of friends, outgoing but caring and compassionate.

The Millers' kids had left home, and the Millers were just about to move into the "empty-nest stage." Stephanie described their relationship as being best friends, and they were looking forward to the next stage of their lives. They were a solid couple and loved spending time together.

Friends described Stephanie and Paul as having a great marriage, and they had just finished renovating a house they had bought four years before. Stephanie had a permanent teaching job confirmed in September 2018, and Paul had a raise at work. With the children leaving home and their work news, this was an ideal trip to have their first vacation just as a couple to celebrate their twenty-sixth wedding anniversary.

Paul was always on the go and certainly not a couch potato and loved getting out in nature, especially with his camera. He was in great shape and never had any medical conditions, with no family history of health problems.

The Millers were getting ready to leave their hotel room in Motel 6, in Twentynine Palms, on July 13, 2018, but Paul wanted to take one more short hike in the hope of taking some pictures of some bighorn sheep. July 13 was the last day of their trip.

He left the hotel alone at around 9 a.m. and drove to the 49 Palms Oasis Trail in Joshua Tree National Park. Paul promised Stephanie to be back later that morning.

Stephanie was going to accompany her husband on the morning hike, but with time constraints pressuring them on the morning of their last day, she decided to stay at the hotel and pack up their belongings. Checkout at the hotel was 11 a.m. (actually 12 noon). They had gone to have a leisurely breakfast at Denny's that morning. Stephanie was also a slower hiker than Paul, and they had both hiked in Joshua on July 12, so, reluctantly, he decided to go on the solo hike.

The motel was very close to the trail, and Paul was sure he could do the hike and return within a couple of hours, as they had to be in Vegas to catch the flight back to Ontario.

Paul was wearing dark shorts, dark gray, almost black Hi-Tec Altitude VI WP hiking boots, a black hat, and carrying sunglasses, a CamelBak hydration pack, and a Nikon D5300 camera.

The 49 Palms Oasis Trail at Joshua National Park is an American national park in southeastern California, east of Los Angeles and San Bernardino, near Palm Springs, covering a total of 790,636 acres. It is named for the Joshua trees (*Yucca brevifolia*) native to the Mojave Desert. Originally declared a national monument in 1936, Joshua Tree was redesignated as a national park in 1994 when the US Congress passed the California Desert Protection Act.

According to the NPS, "The 49 Palms Oasis Trail offers a three-mile round-trip hike to a fan palm oasis. It requires two to three hours and is rated moderately strenuous, ascending about three hundred feet each way. This well-maintained trail climbs to a ridge where large numbers of barrel cacti dot the landscape. After winding around the ridge top, the trail descends steeply to the oasis located in a rocky canyon. Towering palms create a canopy over clear pools of water. Large boulders provide a place to rest and enjoy the sights and sounds of this small ecosystem."

George Land from the NPS said, "It's not a real difficult trail. You go in and come out the same way. However, it is a little bit of a rigorous trail."

When Paul hadn't returned by 11 a.m., his wife grew concerned, but decided to give him another hour and didn't want to worry anyone unnecessarily.

At noon, when Stephanie had still not heard from Paul, she called national park officials at Joshua, and rangers began a search immediately by walking the trail. By 2 p.m. a full search and rescue operation had begun.

At first, the park wasn't too concerned, as Paul was only one and a half hours late, and missing visitors often turned up after a couple of hours.

Paul's rental car was quickly found at the 49 Palms Oasis trailhead parking lot. His cell phone had been left behind at the hotel, but apparently, this was not unusual for him.

At 4 p.m. the washes that lead off the 49 Palms Oasis Trail, the rocky areas, and the side canyons began to be searched and continued to 10 p.m. that first day.

For five days the search for Paul continued in the park, involving six hundred people putting in six thousand hours in total (ninety people at peak), up to twenty dog teams, an ATV search team and a helicopter.

The San Bernardino County Sheriff's Department deputies, detectives, search and rescue and emergency services; the California Rescue Dog Association; Nevada Search and Rescue; and the National Park Service with personnel from the Investigative Services Branch, Mojave National Preserve, Death Valley National Park, Santa Monica Mountains National Recreation Area and Joshua Tree National Park all participated in the search. Due to steep ravines and cliffs, technical specialists with high-angle rescue skills were also deployed.

But no sign of Paul was located, and no other evidence other than his car that he was in the park, such as his camera, turned up. Park Superintendent David Smith said that, "We have a witness who saw, (Miller) at the trailhead that morning, but that's all."

Another visitor from England at the park reported seeing Paul at around 9 a.m., walking quickly and with purpose, about halfway down the trail, he was resting by a rock that offered some shade. The witness reported seeing one other vehicle, with two women and two men in their twenties who went in after Paul down the trail, but authorities have been unable to locate it. There was no camera at the parking lot at the park at the time of the disappearance.

Despite a large number of K9 teams, the dogs were unable to pick up a scent. In high temperatures in the park at that time of year, it can be hard to detect scent.

One of the dogs even had the pads of its feet burnt. Because of the high heat, infrared FLIR detection using helicopters was also not possible, as the rocks are warmer than a human body.

The search was scaled back after five days of intensive search on July 18. The probability of Paul's survival in the extreme heat was low, and park authorities decided to scale back the official search.

Park Superintendent Smith said as of mid-August 2018 there were no new clues as to what had happened to Paul Miller, stating, "I assure them, the park service will not forget about Mr. Miller. We are doing all that we can. The FBI is called in only if there is a murder or homicide and at this point, there is no indication that is the case... nothing to indicate this was a planned disappearance."

Stephanie said, "Maybe he finished the trail and came out and something happened. We really don't know. But if they can't find him in the park, then what's to say he's not out of the park?"

In late December 2019, the NPS and San Bernardino County Sheriff's Department reported they were investigating the discovery of human remains found in a remote and rocky portion of Joshua Tree National Park.

Park authorities were alerted about possible

evidence of human remains after another agency was analyzing photographs of the area taken by drone in November.

Park rangers hiked to the 49 Palms Oasis area and found the remains and personal belongings away from any trails. No identification was found with the remains, which appeared to have been in the area for some time. They reported no initial signs of foul play were found.

In mid-January 2020, official identification of the remains found at the end of 2019 was made and confirmed to be that of Paul Miller.

Another puzzling and sad US national park solo-hike death, showing the dangers of hiking alone, even on apparently safe and well-marked trails.

Paul was an avid outdoorsman and experienced hiker. It was hot out there in Joshua in July 2018, but he had plenty of water on a well-established trail, hiking in the cooler part of the day. He appeared to be well prepared, but in a rush to get back to Stephanie and to leave the area, as it was the end of their vacation.

Paul's remains and personal belongings were found away from any trails, so it appears he got lost and disorientated in the heat and was succumbing to hyperthermia.

It gets very hot in Joshua in July, and perhaps he

sought shade by wandering off-trail? He was wearing hiking boots, and the trail was well marked.

Maybe he walked off the trail to relieve himself, stumbled, and fell, hitting his head against a rock?

There are plenty of steep ridges in Joshua, and Paul may have tried to take a picture of the wildlife and fallen off the cliff edge?

Was it a medical emergency?

Did he meet someone on the trail who caused him to run for safety?

Trail cameras are planned to be installed by the Joshua Tree park authorities, as well as one at the parking lot at the trailhead.

CHAPTER SEVEN

HAUNTED JOSHUA TREE

THE GHOST OF THE GRIEVOUS ANGEL: AN ATTEMPT TO CONTACT THE SPIRIT OF COSMIC COUNTRY-ROCK LEGEND GRAM PARSONS
(**STEVE'S JOSHUA TREE Encounter**)

Joshua Tree National Park (formerly Joshua Tree National Monument), and to a much greater extent the entire surrounding Mojave Desert, has always seemed to have a creepy, morbid vibe. In the early 1900s, it was well known as a desolate, lawless place where it wasn't at all unusual for miners (gold and otherwise) to frequently kill each other over their claims. Later, in the 1960s, none other than Charles Manson fed the minds of his

"Family" of followers with copious amounts of acid and then preached tales of pending apocalyptic doom straight into their subconscious at nearby Barker Ranch in Death Valley National Park. And then, not too awful much later in 1973, Gram Parsons' pals hauled the dead singer's body and casket out to Joshua Tree, doused it with gasoline, and set it ablaze to "release his soul," based on a prior pact, as we shall see below. Death seems both drawn to and to hang over this desert, so it should come as little to no surprise that bodies are constantly being found and/or dug up here with alarming regularity.

Joshua Tree National Park, for all its dark history and strange goings-on, has long since been a magnet for cults, show-business types, and assorted hangers-on from both groups. Singer-songwriter and founding member of country-rock band the Eagles, Bernie Leadon once quipped, "Joshua Tree is everybody's power spot." Indeed.

Several years ago, while living in Las Vegas, I found myself with a few days off and decided to make the trip to Joshua Tree National Park in the California desert, a scant three-hour drive of approximately 187 miles. The trip was to serve a dual purpose—I not only wanted to spend a couple of days knocking around the park, but I'd managed to wrangle a room at the famed and legendary Joshua Tree Inn, a quiet desert hideaway on Twentynine Palms Highway about 140 miles east of Los Angeles.

The inn has long been a favorite of several show-business personalities, including John Wayne. Its simple attractions, besides the peace and quiet, are a swimming pool and a sweeping view of the surrounding desert country.

First, a little background on Gram is in order.

According to Wikipedia, Ingram Cecil Connor III (born November 5, 1946), known professionally as Gram Parsons, was an American singer, songwriter, guitarist, and pianist. Parsons recorded as a solo artist and with the International Submarine Band, the Byrds, and the Flying Burrito Brothers. He popularized what he called "Cosmic American Music," a hybrid of country, rhythm and blues, soul, folk, and rock.

Parsons was born in Winter Haven, Florida, and developed an interest in country music while attending Harvard University. He founded the International Submarine Band in 1966, but the group disbanded prior to the 1968 release of its debut album, *Safe at Home*. Parsons joined the Byrds in early 1968 and played a pivotal role in the making of the seminal *Sweetheart of the Rodeo* album. After leaving the group in late 1968, Parsons and fellow Byrd Chris Hillman formed the Flying Burrito Brothers in 1969; the band released its debut, *The Gilded Palace of Sin*, the same year. The album was well received but failed commercially. After a sloppy cross-country tour, the band hastily recorded *Burrito Deluxe*. Parsons was fired from the band before the album's release in early 1970. Emmylou Harris assisted him on vocals for his first solo record, *GP*, released in 1973. Although it received enthusiastic reviews, the release failed to chart. His next album, *Grievous Angel*, peaked at number 195 on the Billboard chart. His health deteriorated due to several years of drug abuse, culminating in his death from a toxic combination of morphine and alcohol in 1973 at the age of twenty-six.

Parsons's relatively short career was described by AllMusic as "enormously influential" for country and rock, "blending the two genres to the point that they became indistinguishable from each other." He has been credited with helping to found the country rock and alt-country genres, later made famous by such contemporaries as the Eagles, and to a lesser extent, even the Monkees. His posthumous honors include the Americana Music Association "President's Award" for 2003 and a ranking at No. 87 on Rolling Stone's list of the "100 Greatest Artists of All Time."

Regarding Gram's death: in the late 1960s Parsons fell in love with and began to often spend time vacationing at Joshua Tree National Park (then a National Monument) in southeastern California, where he frequently partook in stunning amounts of alcohol, psychedelic drugs of several varieties, and reportedly experienced several UFO sightings, among other paranormal events.

"He was always anxious to go there," said Parsons' manager Ed Tickner. "I visited him there once. It was nothing exciting... but he knew every bar and saloon in the area."

After splitting from his wife, Gretchen Burrell, Parsons often spent his weekends in the Joshua Tree area with Margaret Fisher and his road manager, Phil Kaufman, with whom he had been living. Scheduled to resume touring in October 1973, Parsons decided to go on another recuperative excursion on September 17. Accompanying him were Fisher, personal assistant Michael Martin, and Dale McElroy, Martin's girlfriend. Kaufman later declared that Parsons' attorney was preparing divorce papers for him to serve to Burrell while the singer remained in Joshua Tree on September 20.

During the trip, Parsons often retreated to the desert,

while the group visited bars in the nearby hamlet of Yucca Valley, California, on both nights of their stay. Parsons, as per his usual festivities, consumed large amounts of alcohol and barbiturates. On September 18, Martin drove back to Los Angeles to replenish the group's supply of marijuana. Later that night, after challenging Fisher and McElroy to try to keep up with his drinking (Fisher didn't like alcohol, and McElroy was reportedly recovering from a bout of hepatitis), Parsons was reported to have said, "I'll drink for the three of us," and then proceeded to drink six double tequilas in short order. Then the group made their way back to the Joshua Tree Inn, where Parsons purchased morphine from an unknown young woman who was also staying at the inn. After being injected by her in room #1, he went back to his room but quickly fell into a state of overdose. Fisher later said she gave Parsons an "ice-cube suppository" and, later still, a cold shower. Instead of moving Parsons around the room, she put him to bed in room #8 and went out to buy coffee in the hope of reviving him, leaving McElroy to stand watch. As his respirations became irregular and later ceased, McElroy attempted resuscitation. Her efforts failed, and Fisher, watching from outside, was visibly alarmed. After further failed attempts, they finally thought it might be a good idea if they decided to call an ambulance. Unfortunately, it was too late. Parsons was declared dead on arrival at Yucca Valley Hospital at 12:15 a.m. on September 19, 1973, in Yucca Valley. The official cause of death was an overdose of morphine and alcohol.

According to Fisher in the 2005 biography *Grievous Angel: An Intimate Biography of Gram Parsons*, the amount of morphine consumed by Parsons would be lethal to three regular users; thus, he had likely overestimated his tolerance in light of his diminished intake despite his extensive experience with opiates. Keith Richards, a longtime friend of Parsons, stated in the 2004 documentary film *Fallen Angel* that Gram understood the danger of combining opiates and alcohol and should have known better. Upon Parsons' death, Fisher and McElroy were returned to Los Angeles by Kaufman, who got rid of the remaining drugs Parsons had with him by dumping them in the desert.

Before his death, Parsons stated that he wanted his body cremated at Joshua Tree and his ashes spread over Cap Rock, a prominent natural feature there. However, Parsons' stepfather, Bob, organized a private ceremony back in New Orleans and neglected to invite any of his friends from the music industry. Two accounts state that

Bob Parsons stood to inherit Gram's share of his grandfather's estate if he could prove that Gram was a resident of Louisiana, explaining his eagerness to have him buried there.

To fulfill Parsons' funeral wishes, Kaufman and a friend stole his casket from Los Angeles International Airport in a borrowed hearse, in which they drove the purloined body to Joshua Tree. Upon reaching the Cap Rock section of the park, they attempted to cremate Parsons' body by pouring five gallons of gasoline into the open coffin and throwing a lit match inside. What resulted was an enormous fireball. The police gave chase, but, as one account puts it, the men "were unencumbered by sobriety," and they escaped. Another telling indicates that the police did not "give chase", but that Kaufman and friend were presumably arrested for an "open-container/motor-vehicle" violation and/or suspected DUI, and somehow escaped that arrest.

The two were arrested several days later. Since there was no law against stealing a dead body, they were only fined $750 for stealing the coffin and were not prosecuted for leaving thirty-five pounds (sixteen kilograms) of his charred remains in the desert. What remained of Parsons' body was eventually buried in Garden of Memories Cemetery in Metairie, Louisiana.

Back to the Joshua Tree Inn.

Outside and just opposite the door to room eight, there's a small makeshift memorial for Gram, a guitar-shaped marker that has scattered all around it small tokens, prayer offerings: beer bottles, string tied into bows, candles, incense, guitar picks, metal crucifixes, an animal skull, vinyl records, violin bows, a stone angel, warped bark, cowboy boots, cigarette butts and a big hunk of sage that if lit launches a thick, sweet-smelling plume into the still desert air, where it hovers like a ghost. Particularly fitting, I suppose.

Inside the room itself, it's actually on the small side, but stuffed everywhere with Gram Parsons memorabilia: posters for Flying Burrito Brothers gigs, guitar picks with little messages on them, a fan-made painting of a smiling Parsons in happier times, hair sun-streaked and shoulder-length, blowing in the wind. There are stickers of bands such as the Byrds (as well as tribute bands and a host of other unknown troubadours) on the walls. And there's a big mirror that's been there since Parsons died, in which he saw himself for the last time. Indeed, this place is a shrine to Parsons. One feels as if visiting the tomb of royalty.

And on one of the little side tables there's a guestbook, where those who have been fortunate enough to have spent the night in room eight can pen a note to Gram or share thoughts and memories, even bits of song lyrics. Some of the notes are strangely beautiful, not unlike the words that accompany Gram's cosmic music. "Gram," read a note from some random visitor earlier in the year, "I have once again returned to room 8. I still feel your spirit here after all these years. I've spent many a night here, contemplating what lies beyond as I listened to your sad, lonely ghost singing softly in my ear. I'm ready to go when you come to take me by the hand and lead me away. Love, Tania."

I had checked in early that afternoon and then drove my borrowed Cadillac convertible into the village proper in search of some good Mexican food. From previous trips to Joshua Tree, I knew that a restaurant called Castanada's had some of the best Mexican food around, especially the steak quesadillas. The restaurant is a throwback to the "cosmic hippie days" of the '60s and '70s and is a nod to New Age author Carlos Castaneda, an American author, who, starting with *The Teachings of Don Juan* in 1968, wrote a series of books that purport to describe the training in shamanism that he received under the tutelage of a supposed Yaqui "Man of Knowledge" and sorcerer named don Juan Matus. This training relied heavily on such natural "medicines" such as peyote. Yeah, Joshua Tree has that kind of legacy.

After having an incredible meal, I drove back into the national park and hiked to Cap Rock to watch the sun go down. That's one nice thing about Joshua Tree National Park—its gates are open twenty-four hours a day. You can watch the sun set, the sun rise, and marvel at all the beautiful stars that fill the desert night sky during all the hours in between. As with any sky viewing in the desert, the sunsets here have a spectacular, almost magical quality and are not to be missed.

I arrived back at the Joshua Tree Inn and decided to have one more swim as total darkness set in. I didn't last very long in the water, though. When the sun sets at night, it gets cold rather quick—there's nothing to hold all the heat in from during the day. Toweling off and shivering a bit, I made my way back into room number eight. There's a heaviness in the room all the time, but it seems to be more tense and palpable after dark.

In one corner of the room, over near the bed, there's a boom box and a stack of Gram Parsons' music. All the standard record label releases are here, as well as several bootlegs and other rare, unreleased fare. I choose one, basically at random. The CD just happens to be the first Flying Burrito Brothers album, *The Gilded Palace of Sin*. This first album by Gram's country rock group still holds up to the test of time despite having been released way back on the sixth of February in 1969. It's noted for the continuation of Gram Parsons' and Chris Hillman's work in modern country music, where they manage to lovingly fuse traditional folk and country fare with the strange bedfellows of other forms of popular music such as gospel, soul, and psychedelic rock. This seminal work is listed at number 192 in *Rolling Stone* magazine's 500 Greatest Albums of All Time in the 2012 edition and number 462 in the 2020 edition.

When the song "The Dark End of the Street" played, I noticed that the aforementioned pall that hangs over the room seemed to have grown stronger. The air seemed heavy and stuffy, prompting me to open the back door of the room (which leads out onto a private patio) to let in a little of the crisp night air of the desert. Satisfied after a few minutes, I closed the door and flopped back down on the bed as the music continued.

The last song I remembered hearing was "Hot Burrito #1," and I thought of the promotional film (it was made prior to rock videos having come into existence) for the song, in which band members had rearranged themselves and were playing instruments that they didn't really play. Gram was in the top of his form during this era and seemed to be taking many visual cues from his pal Keith Richards of the Rolling Stones, including a scarf around his neck and "aviator" type sunglasses in some of the shots. Keith was also an influence who helped lead Gram farther into the depths of drugs, alcohol, and general indulgence.

At some point, I had dozed off. The CD had finished and began to play again, as I had it set on endless repeat. During the pause between two songs, I heard an odd rapping noise that caused me to suddenly bolt up into a sitting position. I turned down the volume, listening intently.

There. There it was again.

A cool sweat broke across my forehead. "Gram? Is that you?" I whispered hoarsely to the darkened room.

The rapping sound came again.

I almost laughed out loud with relief when I realized it was coming from the room's front door. I walked over to the door and apprehensively opened it just a crack. Staring back through the crack at me were two dark figures, seeming cloaked in black. I eased the door open a little wider and was met with two young ladies decked out head to toe in black "goth"-style clothing. Black leather jackets, black shirts, black leggings, black Doc Martens boots, black-black-black. You get the idea.

"Hi..." one of them said. "Can we come in?" asked the other.

Against my better judgment, I invited them in and turned on the lights. The strains of Gram singing "Hot

Burrito #1" once again softly warbled in the background as the disc repeated its program.

The pair, who I was guessing were in their early twenties, went on to explain that they lived somewhere north of Bakersfield and had taken the pilgrimage down to Joshua Tree on a last minute whim, hoping they would be able to book the room for the night where Gram had infamously passed away. I chuckled weakly and shook my head knowingly. That rarely ever happens. The room pretty much stays booked (I had reserved it weeks in advance), and only a last minute cancellation or an unexpected early departure would allow such a spur-of-the-moment stroke of good luck. The girls further explained that they were paranormal researchers of a sort and had wanted to stay in the room overnight to try to contact Gram's spirit. This caught my attention.

They offered to "buy out" my reservation for a moderately healthy premium on top of what I'd paid to rent the room for the night, but frankly I was more interested in what the pair had in mind. When pressed, they admitted having an assortment of ghost-hunting gear in their vehicle. Intrigued even more, I struck a bargain with them—they were welcome to stay and do their "ghost hunt," but I wanted to stay on as an observer. They readily agreed to these terms and immediately began hauling in their stuff, which consisted of a few battered suitcases and a couple of backpacks.

Within the span of a few minutes, the room was transformed into sort of a ghost-hunting central. They had EMF meters, a ghost box, a digital camera, micro-cassette audio recorders, a Ouija board, sage, sea salt, incense, and the largest collection of candles I'd ever seen in one place. I watched with quiet amusement as they began setting up the tools of their trade.

They began by first opening up both doors and smudging the room with white sage while "visualizing the room being filled with white light" (so they said as they waved their sage sticks around). Next, they ordered anything evil out of the room, telling "it" that it wasn't welcome and could not return, at least while they were occupying the room. I assumed (and hoped) this protection trickled down to me as well. Next, the kosher sea salt was spread across the threshold of both the main door and the back door onto the private patio area. Satisfied that evil had been banished, they closed the doors. The sage continued to smolder as the two girls went about lighting cone incense in little holders, four in total.

Now it was time for the candles. The pair worked together, and soon it seemed as if every available flat surface had at least a small votive candle or tea light burning upon it. The number of candles actually made me nervous. I didn't want to be the guy whose name was on the register for room number eight if it caught fire and took the whole of the Joshua Tree Inn with it, perhaps freeing the hotel's spirit to meet up with Gram's in the dark desert sky. I mentally noted that I had plenty of water on hand and had seen a fire extinguisher in a mounted box just down the walkway outside the front door.

As midnight approached, it was quite an appropriate time for the spooky festivities to begin. In some cultures, midnight is believed to be the "witching hour," the time of night when the veil between this world and whatever lies beyond in the next is at its thinnest. The girls started out by holding a seance with the Ouija board. I sat in a chair in the corner and watched as the two girls sat cross-legged and facing each other on the bed, the Ouija board between them. After a preliminary smudging of the board and a call for anything evil to begone from the "mystifying oracle," they placed their fingertips on the planchette and began to call out to the unseen world that swirled around us in the room. Between the sage and the incense, I could barely see or breathe, but I managed to sit transfixed as the pointer began to move in a lazy sideways figure-eight (an infinity symbol, perhaps) across the Ouija board.

Soon, something came through on the board, and the

girls held a halting, mostly one-sided conversation with the supposed entity. After a few establishing questions and baseline remarks, they asked the spirit if it would let Gram Parsons know that he was being summoned from the Great Beyond to return to the very hotel room where he had shuffled off this mortal coil all those years ago. With a flicker of candlelight, an eerie quiet settled over the smoky room, and shortly one of the girls announced, rather matter-of-factly I thought, in a witchy, whispery voice that Gram was now with us. Or at least his spirit was. The hair on my arms and on the back of my neck stood straight up. Just hearing those words in a hushed, somber tone gave me goosebumps.

It was if the room were suddenly alive with an unseen force. Something similar to static electricity (the nearest known sensation I can compare it to) seemed to fill the dense, smoky air. The room was small to begin with, but now it felt as if the walls were closing in. As the EMF meter spiked, bright flashes went off as one of the girls snapped seemingly random pictures with the digital camera. The ghost box, which had previously been simply emitting a steady stream of white noise in the form of a low hiss, now began to squawk loudly. It was only bits and pieces at first, but then a very clear word (perhaps an EVP?) came through. A single word: "Cold."

I held my breath as the girls began to implore the box to continue talking to us. The next bit seemed to be an intelligent response to the former word. "I'm cold," came a very clear voice. I immediately remembered the attempts to revive Gram. The cold shower to which he didn't respond. The "ice-cube suppository," which did rouse him a bit. I shivered in the dark. I, too, seemed to feel the cold the disembodied voice was describing.

The ghost box made a few more squawks and farts and unintelligible noises that could have been syllables of speech or some type of vocal sounds, but nothing as clear as the "cold" and "I'm cold" that had been emitted from it earlier. After a couple of minutes of this, the box then fell silent save for the return of the low hiss of white noise.

The atmosphere in the room changed as well. The "static electricity" like sensation I had felt earlier was gone. The room, having felt vibrant and alive only minutes before, now felt dead and musty. Like Elvis before him, Gram had left the building.

The goth girls felt this change as well. They turned on the lights; then one began to extinguish candles while the other put out the sage and the incense, opening both doors and fanning them to rid the room of the sweet, smoky odor. I was impressed with what had just occurred. We (really, they) had contacted *something*, whether it be the spirit of Gram Parsons himself or some familiar spirit that had flown in on the dark desert night air.

At this point, I no longer wanted to spend the night in the room. It felt like I was intruding, like one might feel when opening a tomb and then deciding to spend the night inside. I explained my predicament to the young ladies as they scoured through their evidence, which consisted of a few dozen blurry digital photos and the weird, disembodied voice from the ghost box, which they had captured on their tiny cassette recorders. Even in the now well-lit room, the "voice" had an eerie, ethereal quality. I needed to get out of there.

They understood how I felt and were almost giddy with delight when I handed them the legendary key to the legendary room, emblazoned with the number eight. I figured, hell, I'd trusted them with my very life letting them in the room in the first place—might as well trust them with the room itself. Plus, it wasn't like one can run up a huge room service bill here at the Joshua Tree Inn. It just ain't that kinda place.

I took the lone bag I'd brought with me and tossed it in the back of my borrowed Cadillac. The pair of goth girls waved goodbye from the door of number 8 as I let the top down and pointed the nose of the beast of a car into the crisp desert night and towards Las Vegas.

Rest in peace, Gram. I hope we didn't disturb you.

The Joshua Tree Inn is located at 61259 Twentynine Palms Highway, Joshua Tree, CA 92252. Advance reservations are recommended, especially if you want Gram's room (or any other of the celebrity rooms. Call: (760) 366-1188 or visit them on the web at https://www.joshuatreeinn.com/

PART 3
MOUNT SHASTA

While technically not a national park, I've decided to include it anyway. In this section we'll delve into the mysteries and weird goings-on in what has to be one of the strangest places in all of the State of California. Now, while researching and writing this portion of the book, I was a little bit hesitant at first to recount some of the bizarre stories being found, because some of these accounts are just so far out there and bizarre.

However, after giving it some careful consideration in the broader scope of things, I realized that in a world where people can literally turn a corner on a mountain trail and seemingly disappear from the face of the earth while leaving absolutely no trace in the process (and we have such disappearances from Mount Shasta, as we shall see ahead), well, then maybe some of these stories and legends aren't as far-fetched as I had first perceived.

With that said, let's begin, shall we?

CHAPTER EIGHT

LEGENDS & MYSTERIES

Mount Shasta—just the very name conjures up vague memories of strange tales with most people who are interested in these arcane and esoteric reports of weird activity. Very few places in the United States are completely steeped in mystery and the supernatural as Mount Shasta is.

Located in Northern California, only about an hour from the Oregon border, this semi-dormant volcano and the surrounding areas are—according to legend—home to spirits, gods, Bigfoot, aliens, fairies, robots, ascended masters, occultists, hidden cities made of gold, underground bases, secret tunnels, and other strange entities and features. Rising to a height of 14,162 feet, Mount Shasta is an imposing figure set against a backdrop of stunning wilderness featuring the likes of rugged outcrops, scenic vistas, mountain streams, waterfalls, glaciers, and caverns of various size.

It truly is one of the most impressive mountains in the United States. And even though the last volcanic activity was way back in 1786, it's still currently considered active by the USGS. But aside from the beauty and natural grandeur, Mount Shasta has an ominous air about it.

The mountain does hold some dark secrets. Many consider it a place of portals to strange realms of the unexplained. The indigenous people of the area revered Mount Shasta as a magical and supernatural place many, many decades before the first white settlers arrived in Northern California.

One popular native Shasta legend claims that before there were humans on the planet, the chief of the great sky spirits grew tired of his icy home. In the above world, he used a stone to make a hole in the sky and shoved ice and snow into the hole. The resulting mountain was what came to be known as Mount Shasta. Next, the chief of the sky climbed down onto Mount Shasta, and seeing it was barren, he chose to place trees there. And when he walked through the snow, it melted and formed streams and rivers. As the leaves began to fall from the trees, the sky chief used his breath to turn them into birds. The chief of the great sky spirits was so pleased with Mount Shasta that he chose to make it home for his family, not missing the cold from the above world.

The sky chief made a hole in the middle of the mountain and placed the fire inside it to keep his family warm. When he placed logs into this giant fire, the mountain would shake and emit sparks and spew fire, which explains in a supernatural way the volcanic activity, which the natives most likely saw more than once.

Although it's unknown as to exactly how Mount Shasta was named, one popular explanation states that the name comes from the Russian language. Supposedly early settlers from Russia, who lived in coastal California, were able to see the summit of Mount Shasta off in the distance. They referred to it as a *shaztal*, which means white or pure in some dialects of their language. This eventually came to be pronounced and shortened to just Shasta.

Others claimed that one of the local tribes of the indigenous peoples in the area known as the sha tset ka loved it and hunted on the mountain, and it came to be named after them.

Regardless of how it got to be named, nowadays Mount Shasta is a well-known, popular destination and veritable four-season playground for snow skiers, hikers, hunters, anglers, spelunkers, campers, and many others who merely love any kind of rugged outdoor activities.

Mount Shasta is also a popular destination for New Agers and other seekers, Washington Basque in the vibe of the mountain. Currently, Shasta is home to a huge amount of day spa retreats, a Buddhist monastery, as well as a plethora of new age consultants, Zen instructors, and those claiming to be ambassadors to space aliens and ascended masters.

In fact, there's so much strangeness on the mountain, one is almost assured to have some sort of weird experience when visiting Mount Shasta and the surrounding area. Paranormal investigators state, however, that the most unusual encounters usually happen when you least expect it and are far away from other people. Shamanic types, new age seekers and those trying to contact the mothership or be the ambassadors of "ascended masters" may inadvertently disturb the energies on the mountain... If you're looking too hard for a magical encounter, it may cause the truly paranormal events to become hidden away from prying eyes.

According to some, nevertheless, there's been more than enough bizarre happenings in the area to suggest that there are strange powers at work here. In the lore of the Native Americans, familiar with Shasta, the terms for ghosts, soul and life are very similar.

According to these tribes, unidentified flying objects, which may or may not be ghosts, which are often spotted near burial areas and appear as flickering orbs of light, are to be feared, as merely observing them is said to be an omen, foretelling bad luck, or perhaps even death. Also, according to their legends, after death, the soul is said to travel west and rise into the sky and then head into the Milky Way to the world of the afterlife. The Shasta Native Americans believe that singing funeral songs help the deceased spirit on its way.

Also, according to Shasta traditional law, the entire region is haunted with "akski," which literally translates to pains. But according to the natives, these are spiritual entities capable of taking on the form of tiny people and animals who live among the areas many boulders in the lowlands and in the towering summits, and also in the many rapids and other tributaries of flowing water. The indigenous Shasta peoples consider the "akski" to be the cause of all illness, bad luck and death, in the way that many Christian religions believe the same of the devil and his demonic minions. In a similar vein they also believe these "demons" have the ability to jump into the bodies of unsuspecting victims. According to legend, only a true Shaman or medicine man or medicine woman can exorcise away these demonic entities.

In more recent and typical ghost story lore, it's said

that parts of interstate five that run near the mountain are reportedly haunted by various unidentified ghosts, possibly the victims of car accidents, or they may be "tulpas" or thought forms brought about by the indigenous people of the area. Some tribes believe that talking about or merely even thinking of certain dark entities can draw them out and cause them to take form.

The ruins of old Shasta town from the 1800s are nearby, just south of Mount Shasta and west of Redding, California, which at one time was the county seat. The old town area is home to several reported spectral entities, especially in the old courthouse, where it is claimed that at night, the sounds of criminal trials can still be heard.

Another hot spot for ghosts is in the gallows park at the back of the courthouse, where those found guilty were hung and still linger to this day. A pioneer baby's burial spot on nearby old Highway 99, which at one time was a stagecoach road to the area, is claimed by some to be haunted by a particularly evil and malevolent entity.

Some of the stranger stories from the area are based on the Native American legends of Shasta, with the mountain itself being home to several mysterious races of beings.

This includes not only the aforementioned little people, but also tribes of reptilians and large malevolent humanoids known as the "shupjits," who legend says live in the area of Flume Creek and secretly traverse the lava tunnels to the summit of Mount Shasta. The early white settlers in the area also told tales of encountering the tunnel-traveling giants, referring to them as the Lemurians.

The concept of Lemuria originally began as a rumored lost continent in the Indian Ocean from a somewhat scientific theory, which explained how lemurs were able to migrate to India from Madagascar. Some folks, however, including many occultists, and the New Agers in particular, considered it as a lost continent, which was home to the advanced race the Lemurians, who were allegedly the ancestors of the legendary Atlanteans of the other well-known lost continent of Atlantis. Legend state that the Lemurians are giant human-appearing beings who bore some form of appendage on their massive forehead, which provided them with psychic powers.

Stories of Lemurians on Mount Shasta mainly come from a bizarre book called *A Dweller on Two Planets* or *The Dividing of the Way*, which was written in the 1880s by cultist Frederick Spencer Oliver. Within this book (as well as among esoteric texts he authored), Oliver claimed that a secret city, which was glittering with jewels, was located inside Mount Shasta, and he further established a connection between it and Lemuria.

His writings were wildly popular at the time, and his fantastical ideas of Mount Shasta, as well as Lemuria, were referenced and retold in many news articles and other books of that era along these lines of legend. There are also stories of a secret society that lives in the secret city deep inside Mount Shasta.

The secret society is known as the great white brotherhood. That's not because of the color of their skin, but rather the brilliant white light that often surrounds these beings, who also wear spotless white robes. They're said to be a fraternity of spiritually advanced beings, or "ascended masters," who were drawn to Mount Shasta due to the energy found on its peak. The brotherhood allegedly live inside the mountain and travel through tunnels of gold to their hidden temples made of jewels and crystals.

Guy W. Ballard was an occultist from Chicago who ventured to Mount Shasta in 1930 to inquire about reports from another occultist named William Paley, regarding a group of holy men called the Brotherhood of Mount Shasta. Paley claimed to have observed these holy men several times while traveling on the mountain.

Ballard was extremely curious after reading Paley's reports and, along with his wife, Edna, ventured to

Mount Shasta in hopes of contacting the ascended masters of which Pally wrote. Once when Ballard was out on a day hike alone, he paused briefly to rest at a clear mountain spring in the McCloud River valley area. He claims that while resting by the stream, he was approached by a strange young man who appeared out of nowhere and offered him a drink of some creamy, milky liquid from a leather flask. The handsome young stranger told Ballard that the liquid came from what he called the Universal Supply.

Ballard states that when he drank the liquid, it had an immediate electric and clarifying effect on him, making him feel oddly energized, invigorated, and refreshed. It was at this point that the handsome young stranger then revealed his true name: The Ascended Master St. Germain, and then he was suddenly clad in a brilliant white bejeweled robe, making him appear godlike as Ballard looked on in stunned amazement.

Ballard then suddenly noticed that a large mountain lion, which are common in the area, had approached him to within a few feet. Somehow able to fight off his fear of the animal, Ballard stood his ground. It was at this point that something very remarkable happened. Ballard claimed that the mountain lion suddenly became as docile and playful as a kitten.

At this point, St. Germain proudly informed Ballard

that he had passed the test of courage and gave him four small brownish cakes. Ballard ate the cakes and claimed that they further increased the clarity he had received from partaking of the milky liquid he had consumed just minutes before. He stated that these strange cakes further aided him in being receptive to the master's teachings.

St. Germain stated that he had searched several continents for someone worthy to learn his instructions regarding the great laws of life. Now Ballard, his wife, Edna, and their son, Donald, were chosen to be his accredited messengers after a series of meetings with the ascended master. Ballard claims he was able to channel St. Germain's wisdom and plans for implementing the Seventh Golden Age, the "I AM", which Germain stated would bring about a new age of earthly perfection. Ballard further claimed that through channeling St. Germain, he was also able to view his own past lives and stated that he had been George Washington in a previous life. When Ballard returned to Chicago in 1931, he set about putting St. Germain's plans for the new age of enlightenment in motion. By 1932 Ballard and his wife had founded the I AM religious sect, the Saint Germain Press and the Saint Germain Foundation, a nonprofit organization. Ballard, using the pseudonym Godfrey Ray King, began turning out books, pamphlets, and articles about his new religion.

By 1936 Ballard had amassed quite a large literary collection of several books, compilations of songs and affirmations, as well as a periodical magazine. Ballard had no problem drawing crowds that came to listen to him and Edna channel St. Germaine's teaching, and soon schools and reading rooms began to spring up not only in America, but throughout the world. By 1938, the sect had almost three million devotees.

Some wizened skeptics claimed that the "new religion" was nothing more than old recycled occult practices going under the guise of New Age enlightenment. When Ballard suddenly and unexpectedly died in 1939 (although his wife, Edna, claimed that he had not passed on, but rather ascended), many of the previously devoted became disillusioned with Ballard's rather ordinary departure from this plane and stopped attending the meetings. After Ballard's death, the sect also found itself recovering from alleged mail fraud charges.

The I AM movement, although now considerably smaller, survives until this day. The I AM reading room in the town of Mount Shasta offers Ballard's channeled writings, ascended master and I AM art, and I AM musical recordings that are purported to alter consciousness and allow for further spiritual enlightenment. The music has been described as having an ethereal warbling quality that many believe enhances, among other things, psychic abilities and astral travel.

The experiences Ballard wrote about in 1930 inspired many other stories of encounters with strange beings on Mount Shasta. In 1932, Edward Lassner claimed he knew of a group of white-robed people who hoarded a cache of gold and lived at the 11,000-foot level.

And in 1934, a man named Abraham Mansfield claimed he met a whole tribe of Lemurians on the mountain, who revealed to him an extensive network of secret tunnels. Two decades later, spiritualist Earlene Cheney stated that she received an initiation in a secret temple hidden within the deep wood located on Mount Shasta before becoming a spiritual guru. Cheney was something of a Hollywood starlet, perhaps possibly explaining her passion and penchant for elaborate costumes and very theatrical performances, which she used in her new age church and mystery school, Astara, founded in 1951.

Writing in her book *Secrets from Mount Shasta*, Cheney tells how she and her husband were given instructions to go to Mount Shasta during a channeling session in 1952. While camping at Panther Meadow located on the south side at about 7,395 feet, Chaney and her husband suddenly felt led to climb farther up the mountain during their ascent.

Eventually they were met by a strange young man who seemed to know all about their quest and proceeded to give them his teachings. Eventually the pair were escorted into a secret place known as the Cave of the Mystic Circle. It was here that they were also introduced to other adepts, including the ascended master Kuthumi (a "mystical" name taken from the name of the Koot-Hoompa sect of Tibetan Buddhism), who also assisted them with their teaching. Other ascended masters included Jesus the Christ (Master Jesus, who is Astara's leader and light, and it is his inner Teachings which the Astarian disciples follow), Master Rama (interpreted to mean "the Divine Son of Holy Breath," Holy Breath being the combined Father-Mother God). Ra related to the Father of Light; Ma related to the Mother of Light); the Blessed Virgin Mary (Saint Mary, the mother of Jesus, "the lady more brilliant by the Sun"); and Master Zoser (his name was given to him at birth and means "the Holy," for his birth was prophesized by the seers of the day). The pair's lessons climaxed in an initiation in which Chaney claims she was shown the Inner Great Temple at the peak of Mount Shasta, which featured what she described as a great astral cathedral lit from above by a glorious star. She further stated that these sites can only be seen by the truly initiated and remain invisible to the eyes of lesser adepts and mere mortals.

Chaney also previously claimed to have been initiated in a secret ceremony inside the great pyramid of Egypt, which does make her one of a very few select souls on this plane of existence. Yes, indeed. New Agers, occultists, and other enlightened pilgrims claim that St. Germain, as well as other ascended masters and adepts, continue to wander the mountain, appearing to the most sincere of seekers, particularly in the area around Panther Meadow.

These same occultists will readily explain how the Earth is actually hollow and contains numerous secret underground cities. Among them, Telos, where the citizens of ancient Lemuria currently live and are presided over by the ascended master high priest Adama.

MOUNT SHASTA IS ALSO KNOWN for its weird glowing mystery lights. These mysterious floating orbs of light have been reported on the mountain since the arrival of the white settlers and among the Native Americans decades prior to that. The best time to observe the lights is usually from dusk to around midnight and again just before dawn. While indigenous tribes of the area thought the lights to be ghosts, New Agers and occultists prefer to think that the lights are from the secret ceremonies of the Order of the Great White Brotherhood.

The lights have become so well known that they alone have brought the curious to Mount Shasta based on newspaper articles from around the turn of the last century. The lights were observed by passengers on trains that pass by the mountain in the night, and the mysterious lights continued to be reported to this day. Many people who have observed the lights have come to associate them with UFO activity that occurs frequently on the mountain. If you would like to perhaps catch a glimpse of these lights without traveling to Mount Shasta, there are live webcams available online, which offer twenty-four-hour streams over the mountain's peak.

There are literally thousands of lava tube caves known to exist on and nearby Mount Shasta. The strangest one is Pluto Cave, which was thought to have been created by a basaltic lava flow almost 200,000 years ago. The tunnel-like cave was sacred to the indigenous tribes of Shasta and was rediscovered by white settlers during the mid-1800s. As it's very foreboding and can be scary, it takes its name from the Roman God of the underworld, Pluto.

In addition to being called Pluto Cave, it's also known to the locals as Pluto's Cave and Pluto Caves, so be aware that whichever variant you hear of, it all refers to the same place. The cave has garnered quite a reputation in supernatural and occult circles as a place to find extraterrestrials or various entities from the spirit realm that live deep inside the mountain. Recent explorers have reported coming across evidence of sacrificial fires and objects from rituals left behind in the cave of those who held secret ceremonies and vigils for paranormal or occult purposes.

Stories exist about people going insane after spending the night in the cave tube, where they were allegedly confronted by unspeakable horrors. While these tales may be the stuff of wild campfire stories or urban legends, those who have visited the cave do say they find it very frightening and eerie, nonetheless.

ANOTHER STRANGE AREA located near Mount Shasta is in the MacArthur-Burney Falls State Memorial Park. The spot, named Burney Falls, is an amazing natural wonder that pours 129 feet down into Burney Creek. McArthur-Burney Falls Memorial State Park is the second-oldest state park in the California State Parks system, located approximately six miles north of Burney, California. The park offers camping, fishing, water sports, hiking and horseback riding facilities, among other amenities. President Theodore Roosevelt once remarked, while visiting the area, that this amazing waterfall should be considered the eighth wonder of the world. There are also persistent stories of fairies, or the "fae folk," who appear in the mist or just in the edge of the vision of those who gaze out over the falls.

Perhaps these fairies are actually the little people described in Native American legends from around Mount Shasta. It's also stated that these little people will only appear to those who are honestly seeking them for spiritual enlightenment and not just for a paranormal thrill. Burney Falls is located approximately six miles north of the junction of Highways 299 and 89 on Highway 229. As always, make inquiries with the park service prior to visiting the area in regard to current park and trail conditions.

Multiple fairy sightings on different occasions have also been reported near the area around McLeod Falls, which is made up of three amazing waterfalls flowing into the McCloud River. While the both the lower falls and the upper falls can easily be accessed by vehicles, the middle falls (reportedly the most haunted of the three falls) is accessible only on foot. Not surprisingly, the middle of the three falls is also claimed to be the best spot for fairy sightings. McLeod Falls is located on

Highway 89, approximately six miles east of the town of McCloud.

MOUNT SHASTA IS ALSO CONSIDERED to be one of the most active hotspots of north America's UFO activity. Those well-versed in extraterrestrials state that Mount Shasta is a prime spot for visiting aliens, and weird lights are often reported hovering near the area at night and have also been spotted disappearing into the mountain.

Castle Crags State Park, just south of the town of Dunsmuir, California, along Interstate 5 is also considered to be another very active UFO hotspot. The trails in the park lead into strange landscapes of weird jagged rock formations, and it's the perfect location for encountering anomalous aerial as well as other strange phenomena.

THIS PART of Northern California is also full of Bigfoot sightings and encounters. Bigfoot legends seem to be a more modern tale around Mount Shasta, but the stories persist. Gigantic humanoid footprints discovered in 1955 at the 11,000-foot level have been said to be those of a Bigfoot by some or of some other giant (such as those tunnel-travelers encountered by natives and early settlers) by others.

One of the oddest reports ever to come out of Mount Shasta (and just about anywhere else, for that matter) was in 1962. A woman hiking on Shasta claimed to have watched a female Bigfoot give birth high up on the mountain. Others have claimed to see a female Bigfoot breastfeeding her young in the area as well. To this day, new age seekers, campers, hikers, and even loggers have had sightings of these tall, hairy cryptids on Mount Shasta.

THE ROBOT GRANDMA OF MOUNT SHASTA

Quite possibly the most shocking account ever to come off of Mount Shasta, even considering the wild, fanciful tales of the New Agers and occultists, is that of little John Doe and his robot grandma...

On October 1, 2010, three-and-a-half-year-old "John Doe" (because he's a minor child, his identity has yet to be revealed, if ever) and his relatives were camping by a popular fly-fishing location near Mount Shasta. Around 6:00 p.m. the child's parents realized their son had suddenly gone missing. According to Mr. Doe, his youngster was "there one second and gone the next." They scoured the area where he had last been seen in complete panic-stricken horror. After hours of feverishly searching, the little boy still had not turned up. Now even more desperate, the distraught father decided to call local police deputies as well as the United States Forest Service officers. Shortly, help arrived, and search and rescue personnel combed the forest well into the night—yet there was absolutely no sign of the missing toddler.

Five hours after little John had disappeared, authorities found him lying down in the brush directly next to a trail that had been previously searched multiple times by different searchers and volunteers. He appeared to be in a dazed, semiconscious state. Mr. and Mrs. Doe attributed this to exhaustion and were simply grateful their little one had been found and returned physically unharmed. The on-site medical staff gave full clearance, so the happily reunited family were permitted to return home, where everyone's lives quickly went back to normal. Yet, it would only be a few weeks later that the small boy would share a disturbing tale about his terrifying ordeal.

One day little John's grandmother Kathy, whom he called "Kappy," was playing with her grandson.

Suddenly he looked towards her and stated very matter-of-factly that he didn't like the other grandma. Confused, but thinking he meant his mother's mother, she asked him what exactly he meant. He replied no, he liked that grandma, and he liked Grandma Kappy, but he didn't like the "other Grandma Kappy." Now, even more thoroughly confused than before, she encouraged her young grandson to elaborate further. He asked her if she remembered when he was lost in the woods. Of course she did, she stated. It was only a few short weeks ago. She then asked him why he brought that up.

Little John then explained that while he was lost in the woods, he had been taken deep inside a mountainside cave by a woman he thought was Grandma Kappy. She led him into a cool, dark, spider-infested room filled with motionless humanoid robots. Scattered across the floor were dusty purses, backpacks, clothing, shoes, boots, skis, hiking poles, guns and various types of other weapons.

As John anxiously faced his "grandparent" in this creepy cave, he noticed an eerie light radiating from her head. In this moment he realized she was not his real granny, but rather a robot "clone" of her that was very convincing. Robot Kappy then sternly instructed the boy to defecate on a piece of paper, which she had placed on the floor of the eerie cavern. When he refused, she became increasingly agitated and repeatedly requested him to do so. Eventually the grandma look-alike succumbed to frustration and moved on to a different topic. Allegedly, she informed little John that he had been planted in his mother's womb and that he was actually from outer space. Shortly after this extraordinary account, she took the boy by the hand and led him from the cave back outside to a thicket and advised him to wait for help. This was the same spot where little John was eventually located in the brush along the trail and found to be in an extreme state of fatigue and confusion.

Upon hearing this disturbing story, Kathy became outraged and called her son, indignantly demanding to know just what science fiction trash he was allowing her grandchild to watch on television. Mr. Doe paused and remained silent for a moment, then lamented that he had heard an almost identical recollection from little John only a few days prior. Initially the two chalked it up to a child's overactive imagination. Yet the more Kathy thought about it, the more little John's story perplexed her. What kind of TV show would feature some of the ludicrous topics that the boy described? There was no show with a plot even similar that she could locate. What she found to be even more chilling was the idea that she might have some kind of doppelgänger assuming her identity in order to abduct innocent victims in the forests of Mount Shasta.

With those particular thoughts in mind, Kathy decided to share a haunting experience of her own. Only a year before, she had gone on a camping trip within close proximity to where little John's ordeal occurred. In the morning she awoke to find herself out of her tent and facedown in the dirt, with no idea how she had gotten that way. Somehow she had been inexplicably removed from the sleeping bag within her tent and transferred a short distance away. Upon rousing, she felt an intense pain at the base of her neck. Upon closer examination, two puncture wounds were present, and the surrounding skin was red and inflamed. Another friend who accompanied her on the excursion suffered a matching affliction. The pair originally attributed these injuries to possible spider bites.

Within a short amount of time, both Kathy and her travel companion became violently ill. In fact, she was so sick that she could not even muster the strength to pack her camping things. Her mind raced as she desperately tried to recall what might have happened mere hours ago. Only one thing surfaced from her foggy memory: those glowing red eyes. While she was drifting off into a deep slumber, she remembered seeing several creatures gazing through the darkness. At the time she assumed the strange eye shine was produced by a herd of deer or similar woodland creatures. Following this traumatizing outing, Kathy felt completely drained of her creativity and emotions. It was almost if she were suffering from some odd combination of post-traumatic stress disorder, dissociative disorder, and depression. Several months would pass before she felt like her old self again. Admittedly, Grandma Kappy would have dismissed her episode had her grandson little John not come forward with his firsthand encounter.

As WE'VE SEEN in the other sections above, legends and lore pertaining to Mount Shasta have existed throughout the centuries. We visited the indigenous tribespeople who chronicled a fallen race of prehistoric giants that were said to inhabit the region. As well, we've pondered the accounts of others who wholeheartedly claim beings known as Lemurians use local caves as entrances to an underground crystalline city called Telos. Still yet, some allege a large energetic vortex is present within the territory. In modern times there are many UFO and Bigfoot sightings reported. Each year twenty-six thousand visitors flock to this revered mountain from countries across the globe. There have been alarmingly high numbers of curious missing persons cases within this picturesque terrain, as we shall learn in a moment. While little John Doe's incident seems unbelievable, it's important to consider the odd history and happenings afflicting the entire area on around mysterious Mount Shasta. Perhaps an open mind may be the only thing that will finally resolve this age-old mystery.

CHAPTER NINE

STRANGE DISAPPEARANCE FROM MOUNT SHASTA

What follows is perhaps the strangest disappearance to have ever happened on Mount Shasta:

CARL HERBERT LANDERS.

On May 25, 1999, Carl Herbert Landers, a sixty-nine-year-old man from Orinda, California, disappeared on Mount Shasta while making an attempt to climb to the summit. He was accompanied by two friends, Milton Gaines, aged sixty-four, and Barry Gillmore, aged sixty, both of whom he knew from his local running club.

Although a large search by professional and experienced search and rescue teams covered practically every foot of Mount Shasta, no sign of Carl was found. It was if he had simply vanished into thin air.

Carl Landers' friends and co-workers described him as an experienced long-distance runner, hiker, and avid climber who appeared to be in excellent shape both mentally and physically. He had been a daily runner for the last thirty years, doing several miles every morning. At one point he had even completed the Boston Marathon in an amazing five hours thirty minutes. Even though considered by many to be in his twilight years, he still had the burning ambition to climb the highest peaks in every county of the state of California. In fact, in May of 1998, a full year before he went missing, he had climbed Mount Shasta but didn't quite manage to reach the summit. He vowed to return and stated he would absolutely reach Shasta's peak on his second attempt.

The very typography and lay of the land, so to speak, in both the Mount Shasta and Lake Helen areas is such that you would think it would be almost impossible for some to go totally missing and leave absolutely missing and leave nary a trace. There are no obvious crevices nor any dense vegetation or trees that would permit a body from easily being found. Lake Helen was searched thoroughly, as was the forested areas. Search and rescue teams used a grid as their basis, which began at the very base of the mountain and went all the way up to the very peak of the summit. However, oddly enough, human-scent dogs as well as teams of cadaver dogs failed to detect any hint at all that Carl had ever been on the mountain, although it was absolutely undeniable that he had been there at the time and on the day stated. There was simply nowhere that Carl could have physically hidden nor any place that could obscure a body from searchers or dogs. Many locals who are extremely familiar with the mountain and surrounding area could only shake their collective heads in bafflement and disbelief.

According to climbing and hiking experts, a person in fairly good physical condition can readily make the ascent through Avalanche Gulch on Mount Shasta in one day with good weather, even with snowy conditions, although it has been stated that most climbers who are successful in reaching the peak of Shasta do so when they stretch the climb out over a leisurely two days. The idea of going about halfway, then establishing a base camp to spend the night and make a go at the peak the next day when well rested is most common. This also helps one become accustomed to the thinner air at the higher elevation. In fact, the camp named 50/50 was created for this very purpose, although some climbers prefer to make their base camp at Lake Helen. Either way, whichever halfway point is chosen, these are the most successful in summiting Mount Shasta. Incidentally, those wishing to make it to the peak are required to carry a "Summit Pass," which conceivably allows park officials to keep closer tabs on just who is on the mountain above the ten-thousand-foot level at any given time.

According to an article on an online site for climbing aficionados, known as "peak baggers," the route they planned started at Bunny Flat Trailhead, at 6,860 feet, a distance to the summit of Mount Shasta of around six miles or so. This was the Southern (Avalanche Gulch) Route. From Bunny Flat to Lake Helen the elevation is 10,443 feet, a distance of 3.5 miles, and takes the average climber around three to four hours to complete. From Lake Helen, it's a good three-to-six-hour climb to the summit depending on one's technical ability and the weather conditions, and then another two to three hours back to Lake Helen, and then an additional two hours with backpack down to the trailhead. With the figures in place, one can see how daunting the task of doing the entire climb in one day would become. It makes me tired just thinking about it.

For those interested in the specifics, this chart was also found online at a site where those who have successfully summited Mount Shasta compare notes:

Southern (Avalanche Gulch) Route:
Bunny Flat trailhead (2300 m)

Horse Camp (2600 m, 3.5 km), last drinking water (30', 41')

End of causeway (x, 58')

50/50 Flat (1h 30', 1h 35')

Helen Lake (3169 m, 3hrs, 2h 50')

Head straight up Avalanche Gulch to Red Banks, but bear right of the "heart" as if aiming for Thumb Rock (usually, you can see a groove for glissading: just follow it up).

Thumb Rock (3962 m, 5h 30', 6h 5')

Top of Red Banks (x, 6h 55')

Top of Misery Hill (4200 m, 6h 45', 7h 38')

Summit glacier (4200 m, x, 7h 50')

Summit (4317 m, 7h 6', 8h 6')

Coming down takes about 4 hours: 45' to Thumb Rock, 30' to the bottom of Red Banks (this usually takes a while because it's so dangerous), 1h to Helen Lake, 1h 15' to Horse Camp, 30' to the parking lot.

So, the night before the group planned their climb on Shasta, on the night of May 22, 1999, the trio of climbing friends stayed together in a motel. Promptly at 4 a.m. on Monday, May the twenty-third, the trio departed from their motel room, carrying their ice axes, crampons, climbing clothes, and other assorted gear. They were en route to the trailhead at Bunny Flat, an area that at that time was well covered in deep snowdrifts, although it was late May. From there, the trio hiked approximately four miles to a place known as Horse Camp. The next night they made camp at a location farther up on the mountain known as the 50/50 plateau. Below Lake Helen, 50/50 is a popular camping spot strewn with large boulders, where most climbers recuperate for a bit and wait for the perfect light and weather conditions before making their final assault on Mount Shasta's summit.

It was known to the group that their friend Carl was taking a drug called Diamox (acetazolamide), a medicine to help combat the effects of altitude sickness. He was also said to be suffering from moderate diarrhea (possibly due to the altitude-sickness medication) and had to venture out from the tent several times during the night to relieve himself in the midst of freezing, blowing gale winds. When morning arrived, he still complained of not feeling very well, and he struck out from the 50/50 camp location without his friends. He said he wanted to get a good head start up towards Lake Helen, as he was feeling somewhat cold. It should be noted here that hypothermia (from the extremely cold winds) and dehydration (from the diarrhea) are not a good combination even if just hiking, and certainly not during a strenuous climbing attempt. This one-two punch can (and often does) lead to some serious trouble even for the most seasoned of adventurers.

The rest of the group were only slightly concerned about Carl's early departure from the 50/50 plateau to Lake Helen. Carl knew what he was doing and what he was capable of—of this they had no doubt. The lake is actually only a short distance away, about 650 feet or so, just around the side of the mountain from the 50/50 encampment and at a slightly higher level of elevation. The other men stated Carl was dressed appropriately, wearing two or three layers of clothes, including a brownish coat, ski pants, and climbing boots equipped with crampons for better traction in the snow and icy conditions.

Milton and Barry later stated that they watched Carl until he went out of sight around the curve in the mountain. At the time, they had no way of knowing and that was the last time Carl would ever be seen, dead or alive.

His friends packed up and subsequently left the camp around thirty minutes after Carl. They left their kit at the camp, as they intended to check out Lake Helen's weather and snow conditions and then grab their stuff from 50/50 later. But, after a short time, Barry returned to the tent, which was left at 50/50, as he too wasn't feeling well. Any experienced hiker knows that it is not a good idea for a group to split up, and at this point, all three of the climbers were separated from each other.

Milt, therefore, got to Lake Helen on his own, and he asked a ranger if he had seen anyone passing through on the way to the mountain. He replied that he had seen only one person, so Milt tried to catch up, but subsequently discovered he was way too fast to be Carl, wearing the wrong clothes, and he turned back and asked the ranger again but to no avail. So Milt headed back to 50/50 to try to meet with Barry again, hoping Carl would be there. This was around 5 p.m.

Unfortunately, Carl wasn't back at the tent, he had vanished, and his kit was still left around the campsite. Milt then decided to hike back to Bunny Flats at around 8 p.m. and notify the Siskiyou County Sheriff that Carl had disappeared. Milt left Carl's gear behind just in case he turned up at the 50/50 camp whilst he was heading to Bunny Flats.

The Siskiyou County Sheriff's Department started searching the area the next morning, May 26, after Carl was reported missing, on a grid pattern basis, using the National Guard air ambulance helicopter and a CHP helicopter equipped with an infrared sensing device called FLIR.

A ground search was subsequently conducted on ski, horse and foot by US Forest Rangers and Shasta Mountain Guides. They were joined by volunteers from Marin and San Mateo counties, along with others from Southern Oregon, Sutter, Placer and Humboldt Counties. Several members of the Orinda Road Runners, a club that Carl belonged to, also joined the search on Thursday, May 26.

The Shasta schoolyard was used as the base camp for the search initially, but as the number of searchers grew, the location was switched to the airport. The helicopter pilot took professional climbers to the summit, and they descended the mountain using separate routes at different points on the compass. Despite this extensive search, they found no sign of Carl on the mountain. Neither his body, clothing, backpack or other equipment. There were no footprints in the snow and nothing to suggest that he was ever in the area of Mount Shasta.

When Carl's wife was informed he was missing on May 26, she said she'd had a strange feeling when Carl left for the trip that something was wrong and that he was in trouble.

The SAR (search and rescue) effort was headed by a man named Grizz Adams, a veteran of over four hundred search and rescue operations, and during an interview with David Paulides, he said, "In 35 years I've never had this happen to me... we were all over that mountain, he was not on the mountain... we brought canines in, they didn't pick him up... we flew around it, we dropped guys at the summit, they came down all sides, they couldn't find him... they talked to people who were on the mountain, they didn't see him... there's snow around the path where he was and nobody went outside the path..." When Paulides asked Grizz Adams what he thought happened to Carl Landers on the mountain, he replied: "... that's the million-dollar question, he either went up or in—but he's not on it."

In the four hundred operations that Grizz was involved with, only two, including Carl's, turned up with no trace at all.

County Sheriff's spokeswoman Susan Gravenkamp said: "We've just looked everywhere that we can look, and we just don't know where else to look." Above the tree line, the mountain is not hugely steep, with no crevices or steep cliffs, plenty of flat areas; it makes no sense that a man like Carl could just disappear off the mountain.

To this day, over twenty years later, nothing has ever been found, not even a trace of his equipment, and it is assumed that Carl disappeared somewhere between 50/50 plateau and Lake Helen, as no tracks were spotted off-trail. A distance of only 650 feet, an area that is relatively flat with no dense brush or tree cover.

The topography of the area around Mount Shasta

and Lake Helen makes it very difficult for someone to disappear, and there are no obvious crevices, nor is there any dense vegetation or trees that would obscure a body. The lake was thoroughly searched, as was the forest, on a grid basis, at the base of the mountain. Even after cadaver-sniffing and human-scent dogs were used, they detected nothing. There was nowhere for Carl to hide, and locals familiar with the mountain were totally stumped and baffled.

What's more, this was no desolate spot, there were fifty to a hundred people around Lake Helen at the time of the disappearance, and no one saw Carl. The only evidence he was there at all was his abandoned backpack at 50/50. Milt said there was more than a 50 percent chance that something very strange had happened.

If Carl succumbed to hypothermia, he would leave behind boots or clothing, yet nothing has been discovered in over two decades. If he was delirious from the medication, he wouldn't get very far in the area where he was walking. Although there are black bear and coyote, they only appear at lower elevations.

Perhaps the friends were lying and brought up the bag and left it, but a permit is needed to summit Mount Shasta, and you are required to check in and sign. Did Carl lead a double life and had to vanish for his own safety? Was there a plan to make him disappear? Possible, but very unlikely.

The residents of Mount Shasta City said: "it was like the mountain opened up and swallowed him." Maybe it did!—see the story of the Lemurians elsewhere in this section.

Well, there you have it. The strange, strange tale of Mount Shasta, considering all the paranormal supernatural activity that goes on here, perhaps it is no surprise that people have gone missing from the mountain. With the Native American importance of the mountain and the many stories they tell about Mount Shasta, they have a wary respect for the area and probably for good reason.

IN CLOSING

That's it for another volume of *National Park Mysteries & Disappearances,* we hope you enjoyed it and discovered new information.

Yosemite, Joshua Tree and Mount Shasta are many things... expansive, beautiful, and popular with tourists. Yet, they're also frightening, dangerous, and downright deadly to those unfortunate enough to be in the wrong place at the wrong time.

With all that said, we truly do not wish to discourage anyone from visiting these strange and wonderful places. Just keep these stories in mind, stay safe, stay alive, and come back with a camera full of pictures, a head full of strange and beautiful encounters, and feel proud that you lived to tell the tale.

Thank you for reading this book. We look forward to

IN CLOSING

telling more tales of other national parks—many of which are just as weird and fascinating. In the meantime, be good to yourselves and each other, and we'll talk to you next time. Be well and be blessed.

—Steve & Bill

Volume 3
National Park Mysteries & Disappearances
The Pacific Northwest (Oregon, Washington & Idaho)
Now Available

ABOUT THE AUTHORS

Steve Stockton grew up in the wilds of East Tennessee, but now makes his home in the Pacific Northwest, where he enjoys finding all kinds of new, weird places to seek out. As well as the great outdoors, he also enjoys hearing from his readers.

If you have a story you'd like to share for future volumes or would just like to say hello, you can reach him at SteveStockton81@Gmail.com

---

Bill Melder is a best-selling author and notable figure in the True Crime community. Native to the west coast, Bill grew up on the streets of Beaumont, California. It was here he found his first love of graphic design but hidden within his heart was the love of all things morose, macabre, and mysterious.

After the tragic death of his mother (who passed away in his arms), Bill became a nomad in search of a more fulfilling life. On this journey of self-discovery, he eventually found his way to the heart of the Mid-South and settled in Tennessee, where he met his supportive husband, Justin.

Bill created the popular YouTube channel Missing Persons Mysteries in August of 2019 and has been advocating for the missing and their families ever since. In addition, along with creative partner and well-known author and narrator Steve Stockton, he has given people a platform to share their stories and encounters with cryptids and the paranormal on the channel, which has grown to over 100,000 subscribers.

Come join his search for all things mysterious at: www.missingpersonsusa.com

Bill can be contacted via email: NationalParkMysteriesYT@gmail.com

---

Together they own and operate the wildly popular YouTube channel Missing Persons Mysteries. They both invite you to please drop in and check it out: http://www.YouTube.com/MissingPersonsMysteries/

ALSO BY STEVE STOCKTON

STRANGE THINGS IN THE WOODS

MY STRANGE WORLD

Made in the USA
Las Vegas, NV
01 June 2022